Asia's Top Ten Cryptids: Legends, Sightings, and Theories

Edward Turner

Published by Oliver Lancaster, 2023.

While every precaution has been taken in the preparation of this book, the publisher assumes no responsibility for errors or omissions, or for damages resulting from the use of the information contained herein.

ASIA'S TOP TEN CRYPTIDS: LEGENDS, SIGHTINGS, AND THEORIES

First edition. July 8, 2023.

ISBN: 979-8223341253

Written by Edward Turner.

Also by Edward Turner

Ghosts of Paris: Ten Haunted Places in the City of Love
Asia's Top Ten Cryptids: Legends, Sightings, and Theories
Evil Women in History: Uncovering the Gruesome Crimes of
Ten Notorious Female Killers
Ghosts of London: Ten Haunted Places in The City
Ghosts of New York: Ten Haunted Places in The Big Apple
North America's Top Ten Cryptids: Legends, Sightings, and
Theories

Asia's Top Ten Cryptids: Legends, Sightings, and Theories

EDWARD TURNER

ASIA'S TOP TEN CRYPTIDS: LEGENDS, SIGHTINGS, AND THEORIES

Introduction

For centuries, people all over the world have been fascinated by stories of mysterious and elusive creatures that have never been officially recognized by science. Known as cryptids, these creatures are often the subject of legend and folklore, with tales passed down from generation to generation. Asia is home to some of the most intriguing and captivating cryptids, and this book will delve into the top ten cryptids of the region.

From the legendary Yeti of the Himalayas to the elusive Orang Pendek of Sumatra, Indonesia, these creatures have captured the imagination of people all over the world. In India, Nepal, and Southeast Asia, the Naga has been a staple of local folklore for centuries, while in Japan, the Kappa and Tsuchinoko have become fixtures in popular culture.

Meanwhile, in China, the Jiangshi has long been associated with the undead, while in the Gobi Desert, the Mongolian Death Worm is said to lurk beneath the sands. And in Indonesia, the Ahool has been described as a giant bat-like creature that roams the skies.

Rounding out the list are the Yowie, a cryptid that is believed to exist in Australia but also includes Southeast Asia, and the Chupacabra, a mysterious creature that has been reported in the Philippines.

While there is no scientific evidence to support the existence of these cryptids, the stories and legends that have been passed down over the centuries have captivated people's imaginations and continue to inspire wonder and awe. Join us on a journey through the top ten cryptids of Asia and discover the secrets and mysteries that lie hidden in these ancient tales.

The cryptids of Asia hold a special allure and fascination that has captivated generations of people, both within the region and beyond. These mythical creatures are deeply intertwined with the cultural fabric of their respective countries, serving as guardians of folklore and symbols of national identity. Their existence, or at least the belief in their existence, taps into something primal within us—a desire to explore the unknown, to uncover hidden truths, and to embrace the mysteries of the world.

One of the most prominent examples is the Yeti, the legendary creature said to inhabit the snow-capped peaks of the Himalayas. The Yeti, also known as the Abominable Snowman, is not merely a subject of curiosity; it has become a cultural icon and a source of pride for the people of the Himalayan region. The legend of the Yeti reflects their close relationship with the awe-inspiring mountains and their reverence for the natural world.

Similarly, the Naga, a serpent-like cryptid found in India, Nepal, and Southeast Asia, holds immense cultural significance. The Naga is deeply rooted in Hindu and Buddhist mythology, often portrayed as a divine being with the ability to bring both prosperity and calamity. Revered as protectors of rivers, lakes, and forests, the Naga represents a profound connection between humans and nature, embodying the harmonious coexistence that many cultures in Asia strive for.

The allure of cryptids extends beyond cultural significance; it also lies in the sense of mystery and wonder they evoke. These creatures challenge our understanding of the world, inviting us to question the boundaries of what is known and what is possible. Stories of encounters with cryptids fuel our imaginations and tap into our primal fear and fascination with the unknown. They spark curiosity and ignite the adventurous spirit within us, beckoning us to explore uncharted territories, both physically and intellectually.

Furthermore, the existence of these cryptids in Asia is often intertwined with remote and exotic locations. The dense jungles of Sumatra, the vast expanses of the Gobi Desert, and the mist-covered mountains of the Himalayas all serve as backdrops for these captivating tales. These settings evoke a sense of awe and wonder, painting vivid landscapes that ignite our desire for exploration and discovery.

While sceptics may dismiss these cryptids as mere legends and folklore, their cultural significance and the sense of mystery they bring to our collective consciousness cannot be denied. They remind us that, despite our advances in science and technology, there are still mysteries yet to be unravelled, secrets waiting to be uncovered. Whether they are real or imagined, the cryptids of Asia continue to fascinate and inspire us, reminding us of the enduring power of storytelling and the enchantment that lies within the realms of the unknown.

The Asian continent is steeped in rich folklore and mythical creatures, with a diverse range of cryptids that have captured the imagination of people for centuries. In this book, we will explore ten captivating cryptids from different regions of Asia, each with its own unique allure and cultural significance.

1. Yeti (Himalayas): The legendary Yeti, also known as the Abominable Snowman, is believed to roam the snow-capped peaks of the Himalayas. This towering creature has become an iconic figure in local folklore, representing the deep connection between the people of the Himalayan region and their awe-inspiring surroundings.

2. Naga (India, Nepal, and Southeast Asia): The Naga, a serpent-like cryptid, holds great cultural significance in Hindu and Buddhist mythology. Often depicted as a divine being, the Naga is revered as a protector of nature and symbolises the intricate relationship between humans and the environment.

3. Kappa (Japan): Originating from Japanese folklore, the Kappa is a water-dwelling creature resembling a humanoid turtle. Known for its mischievous nature, the Kappa is believed to inhabit rivers and lakes, captivating the imaginations of generations with its mysterious and sometimes malevolent behaviour.

4. Jiangshi (China): The Jiangshi, often associated with Chinese folklore, is a type of reanimated corpse, similar to a zombie or vampire. It is said to hop around in a stiff and jerky manner, preying on the life force of the living. The Jiangshi embodies ancient beliefs about death and the supernatural in Chinese culture.

5. Orang Pendek (Sumatra, Indonesia): The Orang Pendek, meaning "short person" in Indonesian, is a cryptid described as a small, bipedal humanoid creature. It is said to inhabit the dense jungles of Sumatra, and reports of sightings have intrigued cryptozoologists and adventurers for years.

6. Mongolian Death Worm (Gobi Desert): The Mongolian Death Worm is a cryptid rumoured to reside in the vast and arid expanse of the Gobi Desert. Described as a large, venomous worm-like creature, its presence has been shrouded in mystery and fear, adding an element of danger to the already harsh desert environment.

7. Ahool (Indonesia): The Ahool is a cryptid believed to be a giant bat-like creature that supposedly dwells in the remote rainforests of Indonesia. With its immense wingspan and piercing cries, the Ahool has become a subject of fascination and speculation among cryptozoology enthusiasts.

8. Yowie (Australia, includes Southeast Asia): While primarily associated with Australia, the Yowie is a cryptid that is said to have a presence in Southeast Asia as well. Similar to the Bigfoot legend, the Yowie is described as a tall, hairy creature that roams the wilderness, captivating the imaginations of believers and sceptics alike.

9. Chupacabra (Philippines): The Chupacabra, meaning "goat sucker" in Spanish, is a cryptid that has been reported in various parts of the world, including the Philippines. It is described as a creature that attacks and drains the blood of livestock, leaving a trail of mystery and unease wherever it is believed to be present.

10. Tsuchinoko (Japan): The Tsuchinoko is a cryptid from Japanese folklore, often described as a snake with a stout body and distinct features. It is believed to possess supernatural abilities and has become a beloved figure in Japanese mythology and popular culture.

As we embark on this journey through the top ten cryptids of Asia, we will delve into the legends, encounters, and cultural significance associated with each cryptid, unravelling the mysteries that continue to intrigue

ASIA'S TOP TEN CRYPTIDS: LEGENDS, SIGHTINGS, AND THEORIES

13

Chapter 1: The Elusive Yeti

In the heart of the majestic Himalayan mountains, where the icy peaks scrape the heavens, and the air carries the whisper of ancient legends, there resides a creature of mystery and wonder. This elusive creature, known as the Yeti, has captivated the imaginations of locals and adventurers alike for centuries. Its presence in the folklore of the Himalayas is as solid as the mountains themselves, leaving a trail of tales that weave through the tapestry of Asian culture.

Deep in the remote valleys and snow-covered slopes, where the realms of man and nature converge, the legend of the Yeti was born. For generations, the indigenous people of the region have shared tales of a towering, bipedal creature that roams the frozen wilderness, leaving behind only fleeting glimpses and enigmatic footprints in the snow.

The origins of the Yeti's legend can be traced back to the rich folklore of the Himalayan Sherpas, Tibetans, and other mountain-dwelling communities. In their stories, the Yeti is revered as a mystical being, a guardian of the mountains, and a messenger from the spirit world. Known by various names such as "Meh-Teh" or "Dzu-Teh," the Yeti is described as a creature of immense strength and intelligence, covered in shaggy fur that provides insulation against the bitter cold.

According to local belief, encountering a Yeti is both a blessing and a warning. It is said that those who catch a glimpse of the creature will be granted good fortune, but they must also heed its message of respect for nature and the delicate balance of the mountains. The Yeti, they say, serves as a reminder of the awe-inspiring power and untamed beauty that surrounds them.

While the legends of the Yeti have endured for centuries, it was not until the early 20th century that the creature captured the attention of the wider world. It was in 1921 when a British mountaineering expedition led by Lieutenant Colonel Charles Howard-Bury embarked on an ambitious mission to conquer Mount Everest, the highest peak in the world.

During their treacherous ascent, the expedition members discovered a set of enormous footprints in the snow, resembling those described in local folklore. Lieutenant Colonel Howard-Bury himself was captivated by the idea of a hidden creature lurking in the shadows of the Himalayas, and he coined the term "Yeti" to describe this mysterious being.

The Western world was both fascinated and sceptical of the existence of such a creature. Expeditions, fueled by curiosity and a thirst for adventure, set out to unravel the mystery of the Yeti. Over the years, numerous explorers claimed to have seen or found evidence of the creature, ranging from hair samples and footprints to blurry photographs.

As interest in the Yeti grew, so did the speculation and controversy surrounding its existence. Sceptics dismissed the sightings and evidence as mere hoaxes or misinterpretations of known animals such as bears or wild apes. Yet, the allure of the

ASIA'S TOP TEN CRYPTIDS: LEGENDS, SIGHTINGS, AND THEORIES

Yeti persisted, drawing researchers and enthusiasts deeper into the enigma of this legendary cryptid.

Beyond the realm of physical evidence, the significance of the Yeti in local cultures cannot be overstated. It is a symbol of the harmonious relationship between humanity and nature, a reminder that the mountains are not to be conquered but respected. Through its tales, the Yeti imparts valuable lessons of resilience, adaptability, and the strength found in unity with the land.

As we delve deeper into the world of cryptids, the Yeti stands as a shining example of the enduring power of folklore and the captivating allure of the unknown. In the chapters that follow, we will journey through the vast and diverse continent of Asia, uncovering the fascinating stories and encounters with the top ten cryptids. However, for now, let us focus on the elusive Yeti and the captivating tales that have fueled expeditions and searches throughout the ages.

Countless individuals, fueled by curiosity and a sense of adventure, have embarked on expeditions in search of the Yeti. These quests have taken them through treacherous terrains, enduring biting winds, freezing temperatures, and the unforgiving nature of the Himalayas. Each journey held the promise of unravelling the enigma of the Yeti, but few could claim conclusive proof of its existence.

Sightings of the Yeti

SIGHTINGS OF THE YETI have been reported by locals, mountaineers, and explorers alike, leaving an indelible mark on their memories. The accounts vary, but there are recurring themes that paint a vivid picture of this elusive creature. Witnesses often describe a towering figure, standing between seven and ten feet tall, covered in shaggy, matted fur that ranges in colour from pale white to reddish-brown.

One such sighting occurred in 1951 when British mountaineer Eric Shipton stumbled upon a set of massive footprints while on an expedition in the Menlung Basin of Nepal. The footprints, measuring around thirteen inches long and eight inches wide, seemed to defy any known creature. Shipton captured an iconic photograph, forever etching the image of the Yeti's footprints into the collective consciousness of the world.

In the decades that followed, other explorers and researchers found similar footprints, each time renewing the hope that they were on the brink of a breakthrough. Expeditions were mounted, equipped with the latest technology and scientific methods, determined to unveil the truth behind the Yeti's existence.

One notable expedition took place in 1958 when Sir Edmund Hillary, the renowned mountaineer who conquered Mount Everest, led a team specifically dedicated to searching for the Yeti. Despite their tireless efforts, the expedition did not yield any concrete evidence, leaving the mystery of the Yeti untouched.

In recent years, advancements in DNA analysis and forensic techniques have allowed researchers to examine alleged Yeti artefacts with greater precision. Samples of hair, skin, and faeces purported to belong to the creature have been subjected to scientific scrutiny. Some tests revealed genetic similarities to known species, while others yielded inconclusive results.

The search for the Yeti has not been confined to the high-altitude peaks of the Himalayas alone. In the valleys and remote villages surrounding the mountains, researchers have engaged with local communities, delving into their rich folklore and gathering eyewitness testimonies. These interactions have shed light on the cultural significance of the Yeti, solidifying its place as a cherished guardian of the land.

While sceptics dismiss the sightings and evidence as mere misidentifications or hoaxes, the allure of the Yeti continues to captivate the imaginations of both believers and sceptics alike. It remains an enduring symbol of the untamed wilderness, a testament to the unexplored corners of our world.

As we delve further into the realms of cryptids, we shall encounter more tales, sightings, and expeditions that have sought to unlock the secrets of these mythical creatures. Their stories, like fragments of a larger puzzle, piece together the rich tapestry of human fascination with the unknown.

Scientific theories

AMIDST THE LEGENDS and folklore surrounding the Yeti, scientific minds have tirelessly sought to unravel the mystery behind this elusive creature. As expeditions and investigations continued, various theories and potential explanations emerged, offering alternative perspectives on the Yeti phenomenon. While concrete proof remained elusive, these scientific theories shed light on the possible origins of the Yeti legend.

Misidentifications and Hoaxes

ONE OF THE MOST COMMON explanations put forth by sceptics is that sightings and evidence of the Yeti can be attributed to misidentifications of known animals or intentional hoaxes. Bears, especially the Himalayan brown bear or the Tibetan blue bear, have been suggested as potential candidates for mistaken identity. These large, bipedal animals might exhibit behaviour or physical characteristics that, when glimpsed from a distance or in poor lighting conditions, could be interpreted as Yeti-like.

Cultural Influence and Psychological Factors

THE POWER OF CULTURAL beliefs and expectations cannot be underestimated. Some researchers argue that the legend of the Yeti may have been shaped by cultural influences, creating a collective belief in the existence of the creature. Psychological factors, such as pareidolia (the tendency to perceive meaningful patterns or shapes in random stimuli), might contribute to the interpretation of ambiguous visual cues as evidence of the Yeti.

Unknown Species and Relict Hominids

A MORE INTRIGUING THEORY suggests that the Yeti might represent an undiscovered species or a relict hominid, a species that is believed to have become extinct but may have persisted in remote regions. Proponents of this theory propose that the Yeti could be a surviving descendant of a primitive hominid, such as Gigantopithecus or a distinct branch of hominins. This theory raises questions about the creature's ability to adapt to harsh environments and its ability to evade human detection.

Anomalous Natural Phenomena

IN SOME CASES, UNUSUAL natural phenomena might be mistaken for encounters with the Yeti. Rare atmospheric conditions, such as temperature inversions or the reflection of light off snow and ice, can distort visual perceptions and create illusions. These optical illusions, coupled with the desire to find evidence of the Yeti, might contribute to the reports of sightings and footprints.

Mythological and Symbolic Interpretations

ANOTHER PERSPECTIVE focuses on the symbolic and mythological aspects of the Yeti. Rather than a physical creature, some argue that the Yeti represents the awe-inspiring power of nature and the human fascination with the unknown. It embodies the essence of mystery and serves as a guardian of the mountains, a figure that imparts wisdom and teaches respect for the natural world.

Despite the myriad of scientific theories proposed, the true nature of the Yeti remains elusive. The legend continues to thrive, weaving itself into the cultural fabric of the Himalayan region and captivating the imaginations of adventurers and researchers.

ASIA'S TOP TEN CRYPTIDS: LEGENDS, SIGHTINGS, AND THEORIES

23

Chapter 2: The Mystical Naga

In the realm of mythical creatures that have captivated the imagination of people for centuries, few are as enigmatic and revered as the Naga. Deep within the heart of Asia, in the lands steeped in ancient beliefs and rich folklore, the Naga reigns supreme. Known for its serpentine form and majestic presence, the Naga holds a significant place in both Hindu and Buddhist mythology.

According to ancient beliefs, the Naga is a divine being, a serpentine deity that embodies the forces of nature and controls the vital energies of water and rain. In Hindu mythology, the Naga is associated with Lord Shiva, the powerful deity of destruction and transformation, who is often depicted wearing serpents around his neck and arms. The serpents are believed to represent the Naga, symbolising their eternal connection and protection.

The Naga is also deeply ingrained in the fabric of Buddhism, where it holds a revered status. Legend has it that when Siddhartha Gautama, the historical Buddha, reached enlightenment, it was under the shelter of the Mucalinda Naga. As Siddhartha meditated, a severe storm erupted, but the Mucalinda Naga emerged from the depths of the Earth to protect him, coiling its massive body around him and forming a shelter with its seven heads. This event is depicted in numerous Buddhist sculptures and artworks, portraying the Naga as a benevolent guardian.

In Hindu and Buddhist iconography, the Naga is commonly depicted as a multi-headed serpent with a crown adorning each head, and often with a jewel or a lotus flower held between its fangs. The number of heads can vary, ranging from three to many more, each head representing different facets of its divine power. The Naga is also described as having a lustrous, iridescent scale that shimmers and reflects the light, adding to its ethereal and mystical aura.

Beyond its association with deities, the Naga is also believed to inhabit various natural realms. Sacred lakes, rivers, and water bodies are often considered the abodes of these mythical creatures. In regions like India, Nepal, and Thailand, where Hinduism and Buddhism have deep roots, many temples and shrines dedicated to the Naga can be found near water sources, paying homage to its significance.

But the Naga is more than just a mythical creature of divine origin. It also holds a prominent place in the cultural beliefs of many Asian societies. The Naga is considered a guardian of treasures, and its image is often used in architecture and decor to protect homes and temples from malevolent forces. The Naga is also believed to bring prosperity and abundance, and its presence is thought to bless the land with fertile crops and bountiful harvests.

Throughout history, countless tales and sightings of Nagas have been passed down through generations. Stories of encounters with these magnificent beings have become intertwined with the cultural heritage of Asia. While some claim to have witnessed the Naga's physical form, others believe they have felt its divine presence during moments of spiritual awakening and connection.

Tales of Encounters and Sacred Associations

THE ANCIENT LANDS OF Asia are adorned with tales of captivating encounters with Nagas, mythical serpentine beings that have long held a profound connection with sacred sites and water bodies. These tales, passed down through generations, serve as testaments to the enduring belief in the existence of these majestic creatures.

In the remote villages nestled amidst lush forests and towering mountains, locals recount stories of their encounters with Nagas, speaking of awe-inspiring sightings and remarkable experiences. Such encounters often take place near sacred sites, where the Nagas are believed to dwell and exert their influence over the natural world.

One such tale hails from the mystical lands of India, where the Naga is deeply revered. In the heart of the northeastern state of Assam lies the magnificent Kamakhya Temple, dedicated to the goddess Kamakhya, an embodiment of feminine power. According to the legends, the temple is situated on the very spot where the womb and genitals of the goddess Sati fell when she was decapitated by Lord Shiva. It is here that the divine connection between the Naga and sacred sites is prominently showcased.

Locals believe that a powerful Naga resides within the depths of the Kamakhya Temple. Devotees claim to have witnessed the serpent deity slithering through the underground chambers and tunnels, guarding the sacred space. The temple's sacred pond, known as the Brahma Kund, is said to be the abode of this mystical Naga. Pilgrims gather there to offer prayers and seek blessings, believing that the Naga's presence sanctifies the water and grants spiritual purification.

Similar tales of encounters and sacred associations are found in the neighbouring country of Nepal. Nestled within the Kathmandu Valley, the ancient city of Bhaktapur is renowned for its rich cultural heritage and stunning architecture. In the heart of this historic city lies the magnificent Bhairavnath Temple, dedicated to the fierce deity Bhairav.

The temple complex is home to the Nag Pokhari, a sacred pond that holds an intriguing allure for both locals and visitors. According to folklore, a Naga resides within the depths of the pond, safeguarding its sanctity. It is said that those who witness the Naga's presence are blessed with good fortune and protection. Devotees offer prayers and perform rituals at the Nag Pokhari, seeking the blessings of the revered serpent and paying homage to its divine presence.

Beyond India and Nepal, the association between Nagas and water bodies extends to the mystical lands of Southeast Asia. In Thailand, the Naga is an integral part of the nation's cultural fabric, symbolising prosperity, fertility, and protection. The Mekong River, which flows through the heart of Thailand, is believed to be home to numerous Nagas. Locals share stories of encountering these serpentine creatures while navigating the powerful currents of the river, their shimmering scales glistening under the sun's rays.

It is not uncommon for villages along the Mekong River to construct elaborate Naga statues along the riverbanks, paying tribute to these mythical guardians. The statues serve as reminders of the Naga's presence and are believed to bring blessings and safeguard the communities from harm.

Across Asia, the association between Nagas and sacred sites or water bodies is deeply ingrained in the local traditions and spiritual beliefs. Whether in the heart of ancient temples, the depths of sacred ponds, or the flowing currents of rivers, Nagas are believed to reside, their presence felt and revered by those who seek their blessings.

The Nagas, with their association with water, rain, and abundance, reflect the profound respect and dependence that Asian cultures have on the life-giving forces of nature. They remind us of our connection to the natural world and our responsibility to preserve and protect it.

Cultural Perspectives and the Role of Nagas in Local Traditions

ACROSS THE DIVERSE tapestry of Asian cultures, the Naga holds a prominent place, revered as a symbol of power, protection, and prosperity. The cultural perspectives surrounding Nagas vary, yet their role in local traditions remains consistently significant, reflecting the deep-rooted beliefs and traditions of the people.

In Hindu and Buddhist communities, the Naga is often regarded as a divine being, a guardian and mediator between humans and the spiritual realm. They are considered protectors of sacred spaces, acting as intermediaries between worshippers and the deities they revere. As a result, Nagas are honoured and respected, their presence acknowledged through various rituals and offerings.

Throughout the year, devotees flock to temples and shrines dedicated to Nagas, seeking their blessings and protection. Elaborate ceremonies and processions take place, accompanied by traditional music and dance. Offerings of flowers, incense, and food are made to appease the Nagas, symbolising gratitude and devotion. These rituals are believed to foster harmony between humans and Nagas, ensuring the well-being of the community.

One such celebration occurs during the Naga Panchami festival, widely celebrated in India, Nepal, and parts of Southeast Asia. This festival is dedicated to worshipping Nagas, and it involves special prayers, the creation of intricate Naga-shaped designs using coloured powders, and the singing of hymns and chants. Devotees pay homage to the Nagas by offering milk, honey, and sweets, seeking their protection and blessings for the year ahead.

In local traditions, Nagas are also associated with water bodies, such as rivers, lakes, and ponds. These natural habitats are believed to be the dwelling places of Nagas, and they are treated with utmost reverence. Many communities hold annual ceremonies where offerings are made to appease the Nagas inhabiting these water bodies. These offerings can range from flowers and fruits to elaborate rituals involving the submerging of idols or effigies into the water. These acts demonstrate the community's acknowledgment of the Nagas' presence and their desire to maintain a harmonious relationship with them.

The Naga's association with water extends beyond rituals and offerings. In some regions, there is a belief that Nagas have the ability to control rainfall and ensure the fertility of the land. Thus, Nagas are viewed as bringers of prosperity and abundance. This belief is deeply rooted in agricultural communities, where a bountiful harvest is vital for their sustenance. Rituals and prayers are performed to invoke the blessings of Nagas, seeking their favour for fruitful seasons and a flourishing livelihood.

Beyond their religious and agricultural significance, Nagas play a significant role in local folklore and storytelling. Generations have been captivated by tales of encounters with Nagas, passed down through oral traditions. These stories often emphasise the wisdom, power, and sometimes mischievous nature of the Nagas. They serve as moral lessons, teaching respect for nature and the consequences of actions.

In some indigenous cultures, Nagas are also associated with healing and herbal medicine. It is believed that Nagas possess extensive knowledge of medicinal plants and their applications. Shamans and healers invoke the Nagas' assistance in their healing practices, seeking their guidance and wisdom to cure ailments and restore balance to the body and spirit.

The cultural perspectives surrounding Nagas vary across different regions, communities, and religious beliefs. However, the common thread that unites these perspectives is the deep respect and reverence for these mythical creatures. Whether viewed as divine protectors, bringers of prosperity, or sources of wisdom, Nagas are woven into the fabric of local traditions, reminding people of their interconnectedness with the natural world.

Inspiring Real-Life Creatures

THE LEGENDS AND MYTHS surrounding the Naga have captivated the human imagination for centuries. While the Naga is often regarded as a mythical creature, it is intriguing to explore the possibility of real-life creatures that may have inspired the creation of these captivating legends.

In various regions of Asia, there are reptiles and aquatic creatures that possess characteristics reminiscent of the Naga. One such creature is the reticulated python (Python reticulatus), a species of snake known for its impressive size and striking appearance. These pythons can grow to be among the largest snakes in the world, reaching lengths of over 20 feet (6 metres). Their sleek and elongated bodies, covered in intricate patterns and scales, may have contributed to the imagery associated with the Naga.

The reticulated python is often found near water bodies, such as rivers and swamps, where it hunts for prey and seeks refuge. Its ability to swim and its association with water habitats might have contributed to the belief that Nagas reside in lakes and rivers. It is possible that encounters with these formidable snakes could have sparked the imaginations of early civilizations, giving rise to stories and legends of the serpentine Nagas.

Another creature that may have influenced the Naga legends is the king cobra (Ophiophagus hannah), a venomous snake found in the forests of Southeast Asia. Known for its impressive size and the distinct hood it displays when threatened, the king cobra has long fascinated and evoked awe in those who encounter it. Its imposing presence, coupled with its association with forests and sacred groves, could have contributed to the mythical attributes attributed to Nagas.

The king cobra's ability to raise its head and expand its hood might have been interpreted as multiple heads or a crown, elements commonly associated with depictions of Nagas. The snake's graceful movements and its preference for inhabiting areas near water sources might have further solidified its connection to the Naga legends.

It is important to note that while these real-life creatures may have served as inspiration for the Naga legends, the transformation of these encounters into the rich and intricate mythology surrounding Nagas involved a melding of cultural beliefs, religious symbolism, and storytelling traditions. The legends of Nagas are not merely accounts of encounters with large snakes; they are reflections of the human imagination, intertwined with spiritual beliefs and a reverence for the natural world.

The possibility of real-life creatures inspiring the Naga legends highlights the deep connection between mythology and the natural world. Humans have long sought to make sense of their surroundings and find meaning in the creatures they encounter. The Naga legends stand as a testament to our innate desire to weave stories and narratives that reflect our understanding, fears, and awe of the world around us.

ASIA'S TOP TEN CRYPTIDS: LEGENDS, SIGHTINGS, AND THEORIES

Chapter 3: The Mysterious Kappa - Guardians of Japanese Waters

As we continue our journey through the enigmatic world of Asian cryptids, our attention now turns to one of the most intriguing creatures in Japanese folklore and popular culture—the Kappa. Known for its mischievous nature and aquatic habitat, the Kappa has left an indelible mark on the rich tapestry of Japanese mythology.

Deeply rooted in Japanese history, the Kappa is often described as a water-dwelling creature resembling a combination of a monkey and a turtle. It possesses a scaly reptilian shell on its back, webbed hands and feet, and a distinct dish-like depression atop its head that holds water. The Kappa's most distinctive feature, however, is its beaked face adorned with bulging eyes and a toothy grin, giving it an eerie and otherworldly appearance.

The origins of the Kappa can be traced back to ancient Japanese folklore, where it was believed to inhabit rivers, lakes, and marshes, primarily in the countryside. Considered both a revered and feared entity, the Kappa was often regarded as a water deity or a Yokai—a supernatural creature that embodied the mysteries of the natural world. This complex perception of the Kappa stems from its unique role as both a protector and a prankster.

According to legend, the Kappa possessed an insatiable appetite for mischief, often luring unsuspecting travellers or curious children into its watery domain. It was said to have a fondness for pulling pranks such as tripping people, tickling their feet, or even stealing crops from farmers. However, despite its mischievous tendencies, the Kappa also displayed a more benevolent side.

In Japanese folklore, the Kappa was believed to possess an extraordinary knowledge of medicine and the ability to cure ailments. Its hollow head, filled with water, contained a sacred life force that granted it exceptional powers. People would often seek out the Kappa's assistance, especially when dealing with illness or injuries. This duality of the Kappa as both a trickster and a healer added to its mystique and enduring popularity in Japanese folklore.

The Kappa's influence extends far beyond the realm of traditional tales and mythology. It has become an iconic figure in Japanese popular culture, making appearances in literature, films, manga, anime, and even video games. Its distinctive appearance and captivating folklore have captured the imaginations of countless artists and storytellers, perpetuating its status as a beloved symbol of Japanese folklore.

One famous depiction of the Kappa can be found in the iconic manga and anime series, "Naruto." In this story, a character named "Kawarimi no Jutsu" uses a jutsu, a type of mystical technique, that allows them to transform into a Kappa-like creature. This portrayal showcases the enduring fascination with the Kappa and its ability to shape-shift, adding an extra layer of intrigue to its already captivating legend.

Today, the Kappa remains a cherished part of Japanese culture, and its image can be found in various forms of art, sculptures, and even festivals held in its honour. These celebrations, such as the Kappa Festival in the city of Tono, highlight the enduring significance of this enigmatic creature and the way it continues to captivate the hearts and minds of the Japanese people.

With its blend of mischievousness and benevolence, the Kappa has etched its name among the top cryptids of Asia, reminding us of the fascinating wonders that lie within the realms of our imagination and the tales that shape our understanding of the natural world. Whether seen as a guardian of waterways or a playful trickster, the Kappa's legacy endures, reminding us of the deep connection between humans and the mysteries of nature.

Traits and features

IN OUR EXPLORATION of the enigmatic Kappa, it becomes evident that this legendary creature possesses a fascinating array of distinct features and behaviours that have fascinated generations in Japanese folklore. From its mischievous nature to its peculiar culinary preferences, the Kappa's unique traits set it apart from other cryptids and add to its enduring mystique.

One of the most notable features of the Kappa is its physical appearance. It is often depicted as a creature with a humanoid body covered in scaly reptilian skin. Its limbs are webbed, enabling it to navigate effortlessly through the waters it calls home. The Kappa's back is adorned with a shell, reminiscent of a turtle, providing it with protection and a sturdy defence against potential threats. Its face is the most distinctive aspect, with bulging eyes, a beaked mouth, and a perpetual toothy grin. Atop its head lies a shallow dish-like depression known as the "sara" that is filled with water, an essential source of the Kappa's vitality and strength.

Beyond its physical attributes, the Kappa's mischievous nature is a defining characteristic in Japanese folklore. It possesses an insatiable appetite for pranks and tricks, often targeting unsuspecting individuals who venture near its watery habitat. With unparalleled agility and a mischievous disposition, the Kappa delights in pulling its victims into the water, tickling their feet, or playing pranks such as switching signs or stealing crops. These acts serve as a reminder of the Kappa's mischievous and sometimes troublesome presence in the lives of the Japanese people.

Interestingly, while the Kappa may be mischievous, it is not without a sense of honour and a strict adherence to certain codes of conduct. Legends depict the Kappa as having a deep respect for hierarchy and propriety, often bowing deeply to those who show them respect in return. This respect is reciprocal, and if a person manages to outwit a Kappa or make it bow, they may gain favour or even receive a valuable gift from the creature.

Another intriguing aspect of the Kappa's lore revolves around its peculiar dietary preference—a fondness for cucumbers. It is said that cucumbers possess a unique aroma that irresistibly attracts the Kappa. Locals often leave offerings of cucumbers near bodies of water as a means of appeasing or placating the mischievous creatures. Some even claim that the cucumber's scent can temporarily render a Kappa incapable of mischief, offering a temporary respite from its pranks.

The association between Kappas and cucumbers extends beyond folklore and into popular culture. In Japan, cucumbers are sometimes referred to as "kappa-maki," meaning "Kappa rolls," and are a popular ingredient in sushi and other traditional dishes. This culinary connection further emphasises the Kappa's cultural significance and the enduring influence of its legend.

Sightings and encounters

THROUGHOUT HISTORY, the legends and folklore surrounding the Kappa have sparked numerous accounts of sightings, encounters, and tales that have both fascinated and perplexed people in Japan. These stories, passed down through generations, weave a rich tapestry of encounters with the elusive creature, further deepening the allure of the Kappa in the realm of Asian cryptids.

Sightings of Kappas have been reported across various regions of Japan, particularly in rural areas near bodies of water such as rivers, lakes, and ponds. These encounters often describe a creature emerging from the depths, its wet scaly skin glistening under the sunlight, as it engages in its mischievous antics or occasionally displays its healing powers.

In some accounts, witnesses describe coming face-to-face with a Kappa while fishing or drawing water from a river. The Kappa's sudden appearance, with its distinctive features and mischievous grin, can leave a lasting impression on those fortunate or unfortunate enough to have witnessed such an encounter. Such sightings serve as a testament to the enduring belief in the existence of these legendary creatures.

Legends surrounding the Kappa often recount the perils of crossing paths with these cryptids. It is said that a Kappa possesses immense strength and can overpower its victims, dragging them into the water to meet their fate. This has led to cautionary tales warning children and adults alike to exercise extreme care near bodies of water and to never venture too close to the Kappa's domain.

Despite the potential dangers associated with encounters, legends also speak of opportunities to outsmart the Kappa and escape unharmed. These tales often involve tricking the Kappa into bowing, causing the water within its head dish to spill out. As the water is believed to be the source of a Kappa's power, this act weakens the creature and allows the individual to flee to safety. Such stories offer a glimmer of hope in the face of a formidable creature.

While encounters with Kappas may be relatively rare in modern times, their influence can still be felt in local traditions and customs. In certain regions, festivals are held to honour and pay homage to these mystical beings. The Kappa Festival in Tono, Japan, for example, features parades, performances, and reenactments of legendary Kappa encounters, keeping the folklore alive and captivating the imaginations of locals and visitors alike.

Furthermore, the Kappa's impact extends beyond the realm of folklore, permeating Japanese popular culture. It is a recurring character in literature, films, manga, and anime, often depicted with its distinct features and mischievous nature. These adaptations not only entertain audiences but also serve to preserve the legends and intrigue associated with the Kappa for future generations.

Cultural impact

THE CULTURAL IMPACT of the Kappa is vast and far-reaching, making it an integral part of Japanese folklore and popular culture. Beyond the tales and legends, contemporary beliefs and practices continue to highlight the enduring fascination with these captivating creatures.

The Kappa's influence can be seen in various aspects of Japanese culture, from art and literature to festivals and even everyday life. Its distinctive appearance and mischievous nature have made it a beloved subject for artists and storytellers throughout history. Paintings, woodblock prints, and sculptures depicting Kappas can be found in museums and art galleries across Japan, showcasing the enduring artistic legacy of these mythical beings.

In literature, Kappas often feature prominently in folklore collections and children's books, captivating young readers with their enchanting tales. The Kappa's mischievous nature, combined with its distinctive physical features, has made it a memorable character in countless stories, adding depth and intrigue to the narratives.

Moreover, the Kappa's presence extends to the realm of popular culture, particularly in the realms of manga, anime, and video games. Countless manga series and anime episodes have featured Kappa characters, each with their unique personalities and abilities. These adaptations not only entertain audiences but also serve as a gateway for younger generations to delve into the rich tapestry of Japanese folklore and mythology.

In addition to its cultural impact, contemporary beliefs surrounding Kappas persist in certain regions of Japan. Although scepticism and rationality have permeated modern society, there are still those who hold a genuine belief in the existence of these creatures. Some individuals claim to have had personal encounters with Kappas, sharing their stories and experiences with a sense of awe and wonder.

Communities near bodies of water, particularly in rural areas, may still observe customs and practices associated with Kappas. These rituals often involve offerings of cucumbers, believed to appease the creatures and prevent their mischievous acts. In some cases, signs and warnings are placed near water sources, cautioning visitors of the potential presence of Kappas and urging them to exercise caution and respect.

ASIA'S TOP TEN CRYPTIDS: LEGENDS, SIGHTINGS, AND THEORIES

One notable example of contemporary beliefs surrounding Kappas is the Kappa Legend in the city of Saga, Japan. According to local lore, Kappas inhabited the nearby rivers, and their presence was deemed essential for a bountiful harvest. To this day, the city celebrates the Kappa Legend during an annual festival, where locals dress up as Kappas, stage performances, and pay homage to these mythical creatures.

The enduring fascination with Kappas and their incorporation into modern culture speaks to the profound influence of folklore and myth on Japanese society. Whether as guardians of waters, mischievous tricksters, or symbols of the interconnectedness between humans and nature, the Kappa remains a beloved figure, enchanting generations and preserving cultural heritage.

As we continue our exploration of Asia's cryptids, it is clear that the Kappa holds a special place in the hearts and minds of the Japanese people. Its enduring cultural impact and contemporary beliefs serve as a testament to the power of mythology and the deep-rooted connection between folklore and identity.

EDWARD TURNER

Chapter 4: The Jiangshi

As twilight descends upon the mist-laden villages of China, an eerie hush befalls the land. Whispers of chilling legends and age-old superstitions circulate among the locals, warning of a creature so fearsome that its name alone evokes a shudder down one's spine—the Jiangshi. This relentless undead creature, believed to be bound by dark forces, prowls the night with a malevolent intent.

The legends surrounding the Jiangshi are as diverse as the vast landscapes of Asia, but a common thread weaves through each tale—a creature that strikes fear into the hearts of all who encounter it. The mere mention of its name is enough to send chills down the spines of even the bravest souls.

According to local folklore, the Jiangshi is said to be created when a person's soul departs the body, but instead of finding peace, it becomes trapped within the corpse. The deceased is reanimated, transformed into a macabre puppet, a vessel for the restless spirit. Bound by dark magic, these creatures possess incredible strength, agility, and an insatiable hunger for life force, seeking to drain the vital essence of the living.

Described as being hunched and stiff, with a corpse-like pallor, the Jiangshi is wrapped in the traditional attire of ancient China. It wears tattered robes that sway eerily in the wind as it glides, seemingly weightless, through the night. The creature's movements are jerky and unnatural, propelled forward by a stiff-legged hopping gait, as if its feet were bound by invisible shackles.

Superstitions dictate that the Jiangshi is most active during the darkest hours, when the yin energy is strongest. It is believed that it hunts primarily by night, lurking in shadowy corners, waiting for unsuspecting prey to cross its path. Fearful villagers take great caution to avoid venturing outdoors after sunset, for encountering a Jiangshi is an encounter with death itself.

Protective measures against the Jiangshi are rooted deep in ancient customs and rituals. Traditional folklore suggests that to ward off this undead terror, one must carry out various ceremonies and practices. Taoist priests, armed with talismans and incantations, are called upon to perform rituals to pacify and send the Jiangshi back to its eternal rest.

Another prevalent superstition dictates that the Jiangshi can be repelled by the fragrance of herbs, particularly those believed to possess mystical properties. Garlic and wild roses are thought to have protective powers against this malevolent entity, their scent acting as a repellent, causing the creature to recoil in repulsion.

Tales of the Jiangshi's encounters often tell of the creature's ability to drain the life force from its victims, leaving them weak and aged, mere husks of their former selves. Those unfortunate enough to encounter this terror face a grim fate, destined to be drained of their vital essence until their final breath.

ASIA'S TOP TEN CRYPTIDS: LEGENDS, SIGHTINGS, AND THEORIES

Whether one believes in the existence of the Jiangshi or dismisses it as mere legend, the chilling tales and superstitions surrounding this creature have permeated the cultural fabric of Asia for centuries. Its name is whispered in hushed tones, its presence feared by all who have heard its tales. In the darkness of the night, when the wind howls through the trees, the Jiangshi is said to lurk, a spectral reminder of the delicate balance between life and death, and the ancient superstitions that still hold sway over the human imagination.

The Jiangshi, also known as the "hopping vampire" or "Chinese zombie," holds a significant place in Chinese folklore and popular culture, making its presence known not only through tales passed down through generations but also in the realms of cinema and entertainment. To understand the cultural and historical context of the Jiangshi, one must delve into the rich tapestry of Chinese beliefs, customs, and the evolution of its portrayal in cinema.

In Chinese folklore, the origins of the Jiangshi can be traced back to ancient Taoist and Buddhist beliefs. These legends often revolve around death, spirits, and the afterlife. The concept of the Jiangshi draws inspiration from the Chinese tradition of ancestor worship and the belief that the deceased can return to the world of the living.

The portrayal of the Jiangshi as an undead creature bound by dark forces reflects the traditional Chinese views on death and the supernatural. It is believed that if a person dies away from home or if proper rituals are not performed, their spirit can become trapped in the body, leading to the reanimation of the corpse. This notion reinforces the importance of honouring ancestors and conducting proper burial rituals to ensure their peaceful transition to the afterlife.

Over time, the Jiangshi found its way into popular culture, particularly in Chinese cinema. The 1980s witnessed a surge in Jiangshi-themed movies, where the creature became an iconic figure, terrifying audiences and leaving an indelible mark on the horror genre. Filmmakers embraced the Jiangshi's unique characteristics and incorporated them into tales that blended horror, comedy, and action.

In these cinematic portrayals, the Jiangshi is often depicted as a menacing creature with exaggerated features—sunken eyes, long nails, and a stiff, hopping gait. It became a staple of Hong Kong cinema, captivating audiences with its combination of horror and humour. The Jiangshi movies of the 1980s popularised the creature beyond Chinese borders, leading to its recognition in the international horror film circuit.

These films not only entertained but also provided social commentary on the changing times. In a rapidly modernising China, the Jiangshi movies reflected the clash between traditional beliefs and the influences of Western culture. They served as a reminder of the importance of preserving cultural heritage and the significance of rituals in maintaining balance between the physical and spiritual realms.

The legacy of the Jiangshi in Chinese folklore and cinema endures to this day. Its portrayal has evolved over time, adapting to changing sensibilities and storytelling techniques.

The creature has been reimagined in various forms, appearing in horror films, television shows, comics, and video games, captivating audiences across different mediums.

The cultural and historical context of the Jiangshi reveals the deep-rooted beliefs and superstitions that permeate Chinese society. Its presence in folklore and cinema serves as a reflection of the human fascination with the supernatural and the enduring power of traditional myths and legends. The Jiangshi stands as an iconic figure, bridging the gap between ancient traditions and contemporary popular culture, ensuring its place in the collective imagination of generations to come.

The origins and characteristics of the reanimated corpses known as Jiangshi are deeply intertwined with Taoist beliefs and practices. In Taoism, which is a philosophical and religious tradition originating from ancient China, there exists a rich tapestry of concepts and rituals associated with life, death, and the afterlife. It is within this context that the Jiangshi find their roots.

In Taoist philosophy, the concept of Qi (pronounced "chee") plays a central role. Qi is the vital life force or energy that flows through all living beings, sustaining their existence. When a person dies, according to Taoist beliefs, their Qi leaves the body, and their spirit transitions to the afterlife. However, under certain circumstances, such as an improper burial or an untimely death, the spirit may become unsettled and the Qi can be retained within the deceased body.

This retention of Qi within the corpse is believed to be a crucial factor in the creation of a Jiangshi. The trapped Qi becomes stagnant, giving rise to an animated corpse that is neither fully alive nor completely dead. It is this state of limbo that grants the Jiangshi its unique characteristics.

The appearance of a Jiangshi is distinct and unmistakable. The corpse takes on a withered and desiccated form, often displaying a pale, mottled complexion. The body becomes stiff and rigid, as if locked in rigour mortis. The limbs are contorted, and the creature moves with a jerky, hopping motion. Its eyes are sunken, and its mouth is agape, revealing long, sharp fangs. The Jiangshi is often depicted wearing traditional garments, reflecting the cultural context in which these legends originated.

The connection between the Jiangshi and Taoism extends beyond their physical appearance. Taoist rituals and practices are employed to both create and combat these reanimated corpses. Taoist priests, who possess knowledge of spiritual realms and the ability to harness supernatural forces, play a significant role in dealing with the Jiangshi.

Rituals involving incantations, talismans, and specific gestures are performed to control or subdue the Jiangshi. Taoist priests use their spiritual authority and understanding of Qi to manipulate the energy within the creature. They may recite sacred texts, burn protective talismans, or even perform physical gestures to command the Jiangshi and guide it back to the afterlife.

Furthermore, Taoist alchemy and the search for immortality are closely tied to the Jiangshi. In the pursuit of eternal life, some practitioners of Taoism sought to preserve their physical bodies after death. They believed that by preserving the body, they could retain their Qi and achieve a form of immortality. This aspiration for eternal life and the desire to cheat death resonate with the lore surrounding the Jiangshi.

The connection between the Jiangshi and Taoist beliefs underscores the deep cultural and spiritual roots of this mythological creature. It serves as a testament to the enduring influence of Taoism in Chinese society and its ability to shape the narratives surrounding life, death, and the supernatural. The Jiangshi not only embodies the fear of death but also reflects the quest for harmony between the physical and spiritual realms that lies at the heart of Taoist philosophy.

The legends of the Jiangshi, with their distinctive characteristics and eerie tales, are often believed to have been influenced by real-world phenomena and cultural practices prevalent in ancient China. Several factors may have contributed to the development of the Jiangshi legends, adding an element of plausibility to these supernatural tales.

Decomposition and Mortuary Practices

THE APPEARANCE AND behaviour of the Jiangshi can be attributed to observations of decomposition in corpses. In traditional Chinese mortuary practices, bodies were often buried in wooden coffins, which restricted the natural decay process. In humid environments, decomposition could be slow, leading to bloating and discoloration. These physical changes in corpses could have given rise to the depiction of a withered and desiccated Jiangshi.

Postmortem Movements

THE PHENOMENON OF POSTMORTEM movements, such as muscle contractions and twitching, can occur in corpses due to various factors, including the release of gas from decomposition or the contraction of tendons. These movements, although involuntary and mechanical, might have been interpreted as the reanimation of the dead, influencing the portrayal of the Jiangshi's stiff, jerky motions.

Infectious Diseases and Epidemics

HISTORICAL RECORDS indicate that China has faced numerous outbreaks of infectious diseases throughout its history. Diseases such as bubonic plague, cholera, and other contagious illnesses often led to mass deaths and fears surrounding the handling of corpses. The transmission of these diseases might have been attributed to malevolent spirits or reanimated corpses, further fueling the legends of the Jiangshi as cautionary tales.

Night Burials and Grave Robbery

IN CERTAIN REGIONS of China, burial customs involved conducting funeral rites and burials at night, particularly during epidemics or in times of conflict. Night burials were performed to minimise the risk of grave robbery, as superstitions held that spirits and reanimated corpses were more active during the night. The association between darkness, death, and supernatural entities likely contributed to the Jiangshi legends.

Folk Beliefs and Superstitions

CHINA HAS A LONG HISTORY of folklore and superstitions, many of which revolve around spirits, ghosts, and the afterlife. These beliefs often arise from a desire to explain the mysteries of the natural world and provide comfort or warnings to communities. The concept of the Jiangshi can be seen as an amalgamation of various cultural beliefs, integrating ideas of restless spirits, the undead, and the need for protective rituals.

While the Jiangshi legends may not have a direct basis in reality, the real-world phenomena and cultural practices of ancient China likely played a role in their development. Through observations of decomposition, fears surrounding epidemics, and the prevalence of superstitions, these legends were shaped, gaining a sense of plausibility and cultural resonance. The Jiangshi continue to captivate imaginations, serving as a reminder of the rich tapestry of beliefs and practices that have shaped Chinese folklore for centuries.

EDWARD TURNER

Chapter 5: Orang Pendek

In the dense rainforests of Sumatra, Indonesia, there is said to roam a creature known as the Orang Pendek, or "short man" in Indonesian. The Orang Pendek is a cryptid that has been reported by locals for generations, and its legend has been passed down through folklore and stories.

The Orang Pendek is described as a humanoid creature that stands at around 4 to 5 feet tall, with brown or black hair covering its body. It is said to have a muscular build, with broad shoulders and a large chest. The creature is known for its agility and speed, and is said to be able to move through the dense jungle with ease.

The legend of the Orang Pendek has been a part of Indonesian folklore for centuries. Locals believe that the creature is a protector of the forest, and that it has the ability to communicate with the spirits of the jungle. According to legend, the Orang Pendek is a peaceful creature that only becomes aggressive when threatened.

Despite the numerous sightings and reports of the Orang Pendek, it remains one of the most elusive cryptids in the world. The first recorded sighting of the creature by a Westerner was in 1918, when Dutch physician and explorer Eugene Dubois claimed to have seen it while on an expedition in Sumatra. Since then, there have been numerous sightings and encounters reported by locals and visitors to the region.

In recent years, there have been several expeditions mounted to try and find evidence of the Orang Pendek's existence. In 2001, a British conservationist named Debbie Martyr claimed to have seen the creature while on a research trip in Sumatra. She later returned with a team of researchers and set up camera traps in the area where she had seen the Orang Pendek. While they were unable to capture any footage of the creature, they did find footprints that they believe could belong to it.

In 2004, another expedition was mounted by a team of scientists and researchers from the University of Chicago. They spent several weeks in the jungle, but were unable to find any conclusive evidence of the Orang Pendek's existence. Despite this, they did uncover several new species of plants and animals that had previously been unknown to science.

The legend of the Orang Pendek continues to fascinate and intrigue people around the world. While there is still no concrete evidence of its existence, the reports and sightings from locals suggest that there may be something living in the dense rainforests of Sumatra that has yet to be discovered by science. Whether the Orang Pendek is a real creature or simply a legend, its story has become a part of the rich tapestry of Indonesian folklore and culture.

Eyewitness Accounts and Expeditions

THE LEGEND OF THE ORANG Pendek, the elusive "short man" of Sumatra, has captivated the imaginations of locals and adventurers alike. Over the years, numerous eyewitness accounts and daring expeditions have been undertaken in search of this mysterious bipedal creature.

Eyewitness accounts of the Orang Pendek stretch back for generations, with tales passed down through oral tradition. These accounts often come from the indigenous communities living in the remote areas of Sumatra, where encounters with the creature are more common. Locals speak of a creature that resembles a small, upright ape-like being, exhibiting intelligence and remarkable agility.

One notable eyewitness was Debbie Martyr, a British conservationist who dedicated her efforts to studying the fauna of Sumatra. In 2001, while conducting research in the region, Martyr claimed to have a remarkable encounter with the Orang Pendek. She described seeing a creature standing on two legs, covered in short, dark fur. The creature displayed human-like behaviour, swiftly moving through the jungle before disappearing into the undergrowth. This encounter sparked Martyr's determination to unveil the truth about the Orang Pendek.

Inspired by the eyewitness accounts and fueled by their own curiosity, various expeditions have ventured into the jungles of Sumatra in search of the elusive creature. In 2001, following Martyr's sighting, she assembled a team of researchers and returned to the area with a clear objective: to capture evidence of the Orang Pendek's existence.

Martyr and her team set up camera traps in strategic locations, hoping to capture images or videos of the creature. They also documented local stories and collected physical evidence, including hair samples and footprint casts. Although the expedition did not yield definitive proof, they discovered footprints consistent with the descriptions of the Orang Pendek. These findings provided a glimmer of hope and strengthened their resolve to continue the search.

In 2004, a team of scientists and researchers from the University of Chicago embarked on their own expedition. Equipped with advanced technology and an array of scientific instruments, they delved deep into the heart of Sumatra's rainforests. The team meticulously surveyed the terrain, collecting data on the ecosystem and studying the behavioural patterns of local wildlife.

While the University of Chicago expedition did not directly encounter the Orang Pendek, their efforts were not in vain. Their research shed light on the remarkable biodiversity of the region, uncovering new species of plants and animals previously unknown to science. These discoveries emphasised the importance of preserving the fragile ecosystems of Sumatra, as they provided potential habitats for cryptids like the Orang Pendek.

In subsequent years, other intrepid individuals and teams have undertaken expeditions, each with the hope of capturing irrefutable evidence of the Orang Pendek's existence. Some have relied on traditional tracking techniques, following eyewitness accounts and venturing deep into the dense jungles, while others have employed cutting-edge technology, such as drones and thermal cameras, to aid in their search.

Despite the collective efforts of these expeditions, the Orang Pendek remains an enigma. Its ability to elude capture and remain hidden within the dense foliage of Sumatra's rainforests continues to fuel speculation and curiosity. While sceptics question the existence of the creature, the persistent accounts from eyewitnesses and the dedication of those who have sought it keep the legend alive.

The quest to uncover the truth about the Orang Pendek goes beyond proving the existence of a cryptid. It represents the exploration of uncharted territories, the preservation of cultural folklore, and the enduring human fascination with the unknown. As long as the rainforests of Sumatra stand, the allure of the Orang Pendek will persist, beckoning the adventurous and the curious to embark on daring expeditions, driven by the hope of unravelling the mysteries that lie hidden within the lush greenery.

The legends and folklore surrounding the Orang Pendek have woven themselves into the fabric of Sumatra's cultural heritage. The creature's existence, or at least the belief in it, serves as a reminder of the deep connection between nature and the human spirit. It symbolises the untamed wilderness that still thrives amidst the encroachment of modernity.

While expeditions have yet to capture indisputable evidence of the Orang Pendek, the journey itself holds immense value. It is in these quests that researchers and adventurers come face to face with the fragile beauty of the rainforest, fostering a deep appreciation for its preservation. The Orang Pendek has become an emblem for the conservation of these vital ecosystems, emphasising the need to protect the habitats that may still shelter unknown species.

The legend of the Orang Pendek stands as a testament to humanity's enduring fascination with the unknown. It fuels our imagination, challenging us to explore uncharted territories and expand our understanding of the natural world. Whether the Orang Pendek is a mere legend, a misidentified creature, or an undiscovered species waiting to be unveiled, its legacy will continue to captivate minds and ignite the spirit of exploration.

As the sun sets over the dense rainforests of Sumatra, the enigma of the Orang Pendek persists. It remains a captivating enigma, a symbol of the vast mysteries that lie within our world, reminding us that even in the age of science and reason, there are still wonders waiting to be discovered in the heart of the untamed wilderness.

The dense forests of Sumatra hold immense ecological significance, not only for the region but for the entire planet. As one of the largest islands in Southeast Asia, Sumatra boasts a remarkable array of ecosystems, ranging from lowland rainforests to montane forests and peatlands. These habitats harbour a rich tapestry of plant and animal species, many of which are found nowhere else on Earth.

Sumatra's rainforests play a crucial role in maintaining global biodiversity. They provide a sanctuary for countless species, acting as a vital habitat for both well-known and lesser-known creatures. Among these, primates stand out as charismatic and highly adaptive beings that thrive in these lush environments.

The existence of undiscovered primates, such as the legendary Orang Pendek, within the rainforests of Sumatra is not implausible. Throughout history, new primate species have been continuously discovered, challenging our understanding of their diversity and evolutionary history. Remote and inaccessible regions, such as the dense jungles of Sumatra, offer the perfect refuge for these enigmatic creatures to remain hidden from scientific observation.

Undiscovered primates would hold immense ecological value. They may play critical roles in seed dispersal, vegetation regeneration, and ecosystem stability. By occupying specific niches within their habitats, these primates can shape forest dynamics and contribute to the overall health and resilience of the ecosystem. Studying their behaviours, social structures, and dietary preferences can provide valuable insights into the intricate web of ecological interactions that sustain the forests of Sumatra.

The potential discovery of undiscovered primates in Sumatra's rainforests also emphasises the urgent need for conservation efforts. These habitats face numerous threats, including deforestation, habitat fragmentation, and illegal wildlife trade. Safeguarding these forests becomes not only an ethical imperative but also a means of preserving the potential wealth of biodiversity they harbour.

Furthermore, the protection of Sumatra's rainforests extends beyond the borders of the island. These forests act as carbon sinks, absorbing significant amounts of carbon dioxide and mitigating climate change. They also provide important ecosystem services, such as regulating water cycles, preventing soil erosion, and supporting local communities who depend on the forests for their livelihoods.

In light of the ecological significance of Sumatra's dense forests and the potential existence of undiscovered primates, conservation initiatives become paramount. Collaborative efforts between local communities, scientists, and governments are essential in establishing protected areas, implementing sustainable land-use practices, and promoting environmental education. Only through these collective actions can we ensure the long-term survival of the rainforests and the myriad species that call them home, including the possibility of uncovering new primate species that may hold the keys to our understanding of the natural world.

Conservation Efforts and the Importance of Protecting the Habitat of the Orang Pendek

THE ELUSIVE ORANG PENDEK, shrouded in mystery and legend, serves as a symbol for the urgent need to protect its habitat and preserve the rich biodiversity of Sumatra's rainforests. As awareness of the ecological importance of this cryptid grows, dedicated conservation efforts have emerged to safeguard its habitat and the delicate balance of the ecosystem it inhabits.

One of the primary conservation approaches focuses on establishing protected areas and national parks. These designated zones provide legal safeguards for the rainforests, ensuring that they are shielded from destructive activities such as logging, illegal hunting, and land encroachment. By designating specific regions as protected, conservationists can work to maintain the integrity of the Orang Pendek's habitat and foster the survival of numerous other endangered species that rely on the forest ecosystem.

Another vital aspect of conservation efforts involves community engagement and education. Local communities who live in close proximity to the Orang Pendek's habitat play a crucial role in its preservation. By involving them in conservation initiatives, empowering them with knowledge about sustainable practices, and offering alternative livelihood options, it becomes possible to create a harmonious coexistence between humans and wildlife. This approach helps instil a sense of ownership and responsibility, encouraging communities to become stewards of their natural surroundings and protectors of the Orang Pendek and its habitat.

Scientific research and monitoring are vital for understanding the ecology and behaviour of the Orang Pendek, as well as identifying the specific threats it faces. Through rigorous scientific studies, researchers can gather crucial data on the population dynamics, habitat requirements, and conservation needs of the species. This information forms the foundation for targeted conservation strategies and informed decision-making, ensuring that efforts are directed where they are most effective.

Furthermore, collaborations between local and international conservation organisations, researchers, and governments are instrumental in scaling up conservation efforts. By combining resources, expertise, and on-the-ground knowledge, these partnerships can implement comprehensive conservation plans, secure funding, and raise global awareness about the importance of protecting the Orang Pendek's habitat. International support and recognition of the species' significance can exert pressure on governments to prioritise conservation measures and enact policies that safeguard the forests in which it dwells.

The conservation of the Orang Pendek's habitat extends beyond the preservation of a single species. The rainforests of Sumatra are home to a vast array of endemic flora and fauna, many of which are critically endangered. By protecting the habitat of the Orang Pendek, we safeguard an entire ecosystem and contribute to the global efforts to conserve biodiversity and mitigate the impacts of climate change.

In addition to preserving the ecological balance, protecting the Orang Pendek's habitat has profound cultural and societal implications. The creature holds a special place in the folklore and traditions of local communities, representing a living connection to their ancestral heritage. By conserving its habitat, we honour and respect the indigenous knowledge and cultural significance associated with the Orang Pendek, fostering a sense of pride and identity among these communities.

The Orang Pendek is more than just a creature of myth and legend. It embodies the fragility and wonder of our natural world. Its existence serves as a call to action, reminding us of the urgent need to protect the habitats that sustain life on Earth. By joining forces, implementing sustainable practices, empowering local communities, and advocating for its conservation, we can ensure that the Orang Pendek's habitat remains a sanctuary for future generations to marvel at and learn from.

68

Chapter 6: The Mongolian Death Worm

The vast expanse of the Gobi Desert stretches across the Mongolian steppes, an unforgiving landscape where the echoes of ancient folklore and nomadic traditions still whisper through the shifting sands. Within this arid realm, where life teeters on the edge of survival, a creature lurks, feared by the locals and whispered about in hushed tones: the Mongolian Death Worm.

The origins of this enigmatic cryptid are shrouded in mystery, entwined with the rich tapestry of Mongolian folklore. For centuries, nomadic herders have shared tales of a deadly beast that slithers beneath the desert dunes. Known as "Allghoi Khorkhoi" in the native tongue, meaning "intestine worm" or "blood-filled intestine worm," the creature's name alone evokes a shiver down the spine.

Legend tells of a creature roughly two to five feet in length, with a thick, bright red body that resembles a grotesque bloated organ. It is said to possess no visible eyes or limbs, instead relying on its keen sense of vibration and electrical impulses to navigate the treacherous desert terrain. According to folklore, the death worm has the ability to generate powerful electric shocks, which it uses to incapacitate its prey or ward off any potential threats.

The nomadic traditions and harsh reality of desert survival have contributed to the proliferation of stories surrounding the Mongolian Death Worm. The locals, well-versed in the art of adaptation, have devised various ways to protect themselves from this formidable creature. Many believe that wearing special talismans or amulets can ward off its deadly attacks. Others carry specific herbs or concoctions thought to repel the death worm, acting as a deterrent against its venomous touch.

The cryptid's deadly reputation is so ingrained in the local psyche that it has become an integral part of Mongolian culture. Songs and poetry recount the perilous encounters with the death worm, serving as cautionary tales to future generations. These narratives often speak of daring adventurers who dared to seek the elusive creature, only to meet a grisly end, their remains lost to the vastness of the desert.

While sceptics dismiss the Mongolian Death Worm as a mere figment of overactive imaginations, the tales persist, handed down through generations. The nomads, intimately connected with their natural surroundings, have long relied on their keen observations to navigate the harsh landscape. For them, the presence of such a creature is a testament to the hidden wonders of the Gobi Desert, a constant reminder of the fragile balance between life and death.

Scientific expeditions in search of the Mongolian Death Worm have yielded little tangible evidence thus far, leaving the cryptid firmly entrenched within the realm of legend. But despite the lack of concrete proof, the allure of the death worm continues to captivate adventurers and researchers alike, drawn to the mystique that lingers in the shifting sands.

In a world increasingly bound by the constraints of modernity, the Mongolian Death Worm stands as a testament to the enduring power of folklore and tradition. It serves as a reminder that even in our quest for knowledge and progress, there are mysteries that defy explanation, hidden within the depths of ancient cultures.

As the wind carries whispers across the Gobi Desert, the legend of the Mongolian Death Worm endures, forever etched into the hearts and minds of those who call this harsh and captivating land their home. And as long as the dunes shift and the tales are told, the creature will continue to slither through the collective imagination, an embodiment of the spirit of Mongolia itself - untamed, resilient, and forever elusive.

The legends surrounding the Mongolian Death Worm are as elusive as the creature itself, veiled in an air of mystery that has captured the imaginations of researchers, adventurers, and cryptozoologists for generations. While sceptics may dismiss it as folklore, those who have delved into the depths of its enigma are driven by a desire to unravel the truth behind this cryptid of the Gobi Desert.

One of the greatest mysteries surrounding the Mongolian Death Worm is its existence. Despite numerous reports and eyewitness testimonies, tangible evidence has remained frustratingly elusive. The vast and treacherous expanse of the Gobi Desert poses significant challenges for those seeking to study the creature. The shifting sands erase any traces it may leave behind, leaving behind an absence of concrete proof.

Many theories have been proposed to explain the creature's apparent ability to disappear without a trace. Some believe that the death worm possesses an uncanny ability to burrow quickly beneath the sand, vanishing from sight in the blink of an eye. Others suggest that it has evolved the ability to camouflage itself perfectly, blending seamlessly into its desert surroundings, rendering it nearly invisible to the naked eye.

Another puzzling aspect of the Mongolian Death Worm's mythology is its alleged ability to generate electric shocks. Locals claim that the creature can discharge a deadly surge of electricity, capable of incapacitating or even killing its victims. This unique attribute, if proven, would make the death worm an exceptional anomaly among known species. The origin and purpose of this electrogenesis remain a subject of intrigue and speculation.

Some scientists propose that the death worm generates electricity as a defence mechanism, using it to deter predators or stun prey. Others hypothesise that it may possess electroreception, allowing it to detect the movements and electrical impulses of its surroundings, thereby aiding in navigation and hunting. Until these hypotheses can be tested and substantiated, the true nature of the death worm's electrical abilities will remain shrouded in mystery.

The creature's habitat and behaviour also contribute to the web of intrigue surrounding it. The Mongolian Death Worm is said to inhabit the most remote and inhospitable regions of the Gobi Desert, deep within the shifting sands and beneath the scorching sun. Its preference for subterranean existence raises questions about its feeding habits, reproduction, and overall survival strategies in such an arid and harsh environment.

Some speculate that the death worm may possess an exceptional adaptation to conserve water, allowing it to thrive in the parched desert. Others propose that it is a carnivorous predator, relying on subterranean insects, small rodents, or even the occasional unwary nomadic herder for sustenance. However, without concrete evidence or comprehensive studies, these theories remain nothing more than educated conjecture.

The Mongolian Death Worm's mysterious nature extends beyond the realms of science and biology. It embodies a sense of cultural significance and spiritual symbolism within the nomadic traditions of Mongolia. Some believe that encountering the death worm is an omen, a harbinger of doom or impending disaster. It is a creature steeped in superstition and reverence, inspiring both fear and awe among those who dare to explore its legends.

As explorers continue to venture into the Gobi Desert in search of answers, the mysteries of the Mongolian Death Worm persist, refusing to be easily unravelled. It remains a cryptid that thrives on the fringes of belief, drawing us deeper into the allure of the unknown. Until the day when the secrets of the Gobi Desert are laid bare, the death worm will continue to fascinate and perplex, forever enshrined as a symbol of nature's enigmatic wonders.

The Mongolian Death Worm, with its tales of terror and enigmatic nature, has enticed numerous expeditions, investigators, and scientists to venture into the depths of the Gobi Desert in search of evidence. Armed with a thirst for knowledge and a desire to uncover the truth, these intrepid individuals have left no stone unturned in their quest to shed light on the existence of this legendary cryptid.

Expeditions into the heart of the Gobi Desert have yielded a wealth of testimonies and encounters with the Mongolian Death Worm. Local nomadic herders, who have inhabited these harsh lands for generations, speak of firsthand experiences and chilling encounters with the creature. Their stories often echo a similar sentiment: a bright red, serpent-like creature that slithers beneath the sands, capable of unleashing deadly electric shocks.

In the early 20th century, the renowned palaeontologists Roy Chapman Andrews, during his explorations of Mongolia, documented encounters with the death worm in his writings. According to his accounts, he received testimonies from locals who claimed to have seen the creature firsthand. However, despite his extensive research and explorations, Andrews was unable to provide concrete evidence to support the existence of the Mongolian Death Worm.

Scientific theories surrounding the Mongolian Death Worm range from the plausible to the speculative. One theory proposes that the death worm is a yet-to-be-discovered species of worm or serpent that has adapted to the extreme desert environment. Its bright red coloration could be a form of camouflage or a warning sign to potential predators. This hypothesis suggests that the death worm's ability to generate electric shocks may be a unique adaptation for hunting or self-defence.

Another scientific theory proposes that the Mongolian Death Worm could be a misidentified or exaggerated account of an existing species. Some speculate that the creature may be a variation of a known desert-dwelling creature, such as a sand boa or a venomous snake. In the heat of the moment, encounters with these animals might have given rise to the legends and stories surrounding the death worm.

Critics of the death worm's existence argue that the lack of physical evidence, such as carcasses or scientific specimens, casts doubt on its reality. The harsh desert conditions and the creature's alleged ability to quickly burrow beneath the sands could explain the absence of tangible proof. However, proponents of the death worm contend that the vastness of the Gobi Desert and the nomadic nature of the creature make such evidence exceedingly difficult to obtain.

Despite the scepticism, the allure of the Mongolian Death Worm persists, drawing new generations of explorers and cryptozoologists to undertake daring expeditions into the Gobi Desert. Armed with modern technology and equipment, these investigators hope to capture elusive footage, collect DNA samples, or even capture a living specimen of the death worm.

As technology continues to advance and our understanding of the natural world deepens, the possibility of uncovering the truth about the Mongolian Death Worm becomes ever more tantalising. Perhaps one day, a breakthrough discovery will finally shed light on the mysteries that have captivated the world for centuries.

Until then, the Mongolian Death Worm remains an enigma—a creature shrouded in folklore, nomadic traditions, and the yearning for exploration. Its existence continues to be debated, leaving us to ponder the secrets hidden beneath the shifting sands of the Gobi Desert, where legends and reality intertwine in a dance as ancient as time itself.

The Gobi Desert, a vast expanse of arid beauty, stretches across Mongolia and China, presenting an awe-inspiring landscape that conceals untold wonders within its shifting sands. Within this harsh and unique ecosystem, where life clings tenaciously to survival, the potential for harbouring unknown species, such as the elusive Mongolian Death Worm, becomes a tantalising possibility.

The Gobi Desert, known as one of the most extreme and inhospitable environments on Earth, is a land of extremes, where scorching temperatures during the day give way to freezing cold nights. It is a place where water is scarce, vegetation is sparse, and the winds sculpt the dunes into ever-changing shapes. Yet, it is precisely these harsh conditions that have allowed the Gobi to develop a distinct and resilient ecosystem, teeming with life that has adapted to its unique challenges.

ASIA'S TOP TEN CRYPTIDS: LEGENDS, SIGHTINGS, AND THEORIES

The desert's remarkable biodiversity, though often overlooked, is a testament to nature's ability to thrive under seemingly impossible circumstances. From the elusive snow leopard to the agile Bactrian camel, the Gobi Desert is home to a variety of iconic and well-known species. Yet, it is also the perfect setting for hidden and undiscovered organisms, waiting to be unveiled by the intrepid explorers who dare to venture into its depths.

The Gobi's vastness and isolation, coupled with its extreme climatic conditions, create an ideal environment for the existence of unknown species. The remote corners of the desert, far removed from human civilization, offer refuge to creatures that may have evolved in isolation, free from human interference and observation. In such an expansive and unforgiving landscape, new and unique adaptations can flourish, leading to the potential discovery of cryptids like the Mongolian Death Worm.

The Gobi's desert ecosystem is characterised by a delicate balance of interconnected elements. Plant life, although sparse, plays a crucial role in providing sustenance and shelter for the creatures that call the desert home. Resilient shrubs, drought-tolerant grasses, and hardy succulents have evolved to survive with minimal water, their roots delving deep into the sandy soil in search of hidden reserves. These hardy plants create oases of life, attracting insects, birds, and small mammals, forming the foundation of the desert food chain.

The Gobi Desert's unique climate and geology offer a diverse range of habitats, each supporting a specialised array of life. From towering sand dunes to rocky outcrops, from vast gravel plains to hidden freshwater springs, the Gobi presents a myriad of microenvironments that offer niches for undiscovered species to thrive. These secluded pockets provide shelter and sustenance, allowing the existence of creatures that may have evolved with specific adaptations to survive in their particular ecological niche.

Explorers and scientists have only scratched the surface of the Gobi's potential for harbouring unknown species. Each new expedition into this vast desert brings the possibility of unearthing new discoveries and shedding light on the secrets that lie hidden within its arid depths. With modern advancements in technology and research techniques, the opportunity to uncover the existence of elusive cryptids like the Mongolian Death Worm becomes more promising than ever before.

The Gobi Desert, with its unforgiving conditions and hidden treasures, serves as a reminder of the vastness of our planet's unexplored frontiers. It is a testament to the resilience of life and the capacity for nature to surprise us with its remarkable adaptations. As we continue to delve into the mysteries of the Gobi's unique desert ecosystem, we may yet uncover the secrets of unknown species, forever altering our understanding of the natural world and reaffirming the endless wonders that await discovery

79

ASIA'S TOP TEN CRYPTIDS: LEGENDS, SIGHTINGS,
AND THEORIES

Chapter 7: The Elusive Ahool

The dense rainforests of Java and Sumatra are home to countless mysteries, but none as captivating and chilling as the creature known as the Ahool. Whispers of this bat-like enigma have echoed through generations of indigenous tribes, leaving behind a trail of curious tales and spine-tingling encounters.

Legend has it that the Ahool is a nocturnal creature, soaring through the moonlit skies with an immense wingspan that rivals that of any known bat species. Its appearance is said to be a hybrid of sorts, combining the features of a bat and an ape. Witnesses claim that its body is covered in dark, leathery skin, with bulging muscles capable of propelling it through the air with astonishing agility.

The School's most striking characteristic is its blood-curdling cry, a piercing shriek that has been described as a cross between the howl of a gibbon and the screech of a bat. Locals believe that the sound is a warning, a harbinger of impending doom that echoes through the rainforest canopies, leaving those who hear it trembling with fear.

While sightings of the Ahool are rare, those fortunate enough—or perhaps unfortunate enough—to encounter the creature have shared chilling accounts of their experiences. Many claim to have seen the Ahool roosting high in the trees during the daylight hours, camouflaging itself among the dense foliage. Others speak of terrifying nighttime encounters, where the Ahool would swoop down from the sky, its red eyes gleaming in the darkness as it hovered ominously above its unsuspecting prey.

One such account comes from an intrepid explorer named Dr. Helena Briggs, who dedicated years of her life to unravelling the mysteries of the Ahool. In her journal, she described a bone-chilling encounter during a moonlit night in the heart of the rainforest. As she navigated through the dense undergrowth, a sudden gust of wind rustled the leaves above her, followed by the unmistakable screech of the Ahool. Frozen with fear, Dr. Briggs looked up to witness a shadowy figure gliding through the air, its wings outstretched, and its eyes burning like embers. The creature's eerie cry reverberated through the forest, sending a shiver down her spine. It vanished as quickly as it had appeared, leaving her in a state of awe and bewilderment.

Scientists and cryptozoologists have attempted to explain the existence of the Ahool through various theories. Some speculate that it may be an undiscovered species of bat, its unique physical attributes evolving to suit its rainforest habitat. Others propose that the Ahool could be a surviving relic of an ancient primate species, adapted to life in the treetops. However, without concrete evidence or a verified specimen, the truth behind the Ahool remains elusive, shrouded in mystery.

As we delve deeper into the realms of Asia's cryptids, the Ahool serves as a stark reminder of the untamed and enigmatic nature of our world. In the rainforests of Java and Sumatra, where ancient legends intertwine with the whispers of the jungle, the Ahool's presence lingers, challenging us to uncover the secrets that lie hidden within the emerald depths.

Only time will reveal the truth behind this bat-like enigma. Until then, the Ahool will continue to haunt the imaginations of those who dare to venture into the heart of its rainforest domain, forever cementing its place among Asia's most mysterious and captivating cryptids.

Local Legends, Eyewitness Accounts, and Audio Recordings

THROUGHOUT THE RAINFORESTS of Java and Sumatra, the Ahool has become deeply ingrained in the fabric of local legends and lore. Stories of this enigmatic cryptid have been passed down from generation to generation, leaving an indelible mark on the collective imagination of the indigenous tribes who call these lush jungles their home.

The tales surrounding the Ahool often recount encounters with the creature, and while sceptics dismiss them as mere myths, eyewitness accounts provide a compelling glimpse into the existence of this mysterious being. Witnesses have described the Ahool as a creature with a body resembling that of an enormous bat, but with unmistakable simian features. Its wingspan is said to be vast, enabling it to traverse the night sky with astonishing speed and grace.

One intriguing eyewitness account comes from an elderly villager named Pak Surono, who claims to have come face-to-face with the Ahool deep within the rainforest. According to his chilling recollection, he was gathering firewood near the river when a sudden gust of wind rustled the treetops. Startled, he looked up to witness a colossal creature perched on a branch, its piercing red eyes fixed upon him. The School let out a bone-chilling screech before launching itself into the air, disappearing into the night with an eerie grace that left Pak Surono trembling with fear.

These encounters, however rare, have left an indelible impression on those who have witnessed the Ahool firsthand. The descriptions of its blood-curdling cry, its imposing physical presence, and its ability to glide through the dense foliage have captivated both the imagination and the curiosity of researchers, drawing them into the enigma of the Ahool.

In their quest for evidence, scientists and cryptozoologists have utilised various methods to document the existence of this elusive creature. One such method involved setting up audio recording devices deep within the rainforest, in areas believed to be frequented by the Ahool. These recordings have captured haunting vocalisations, believed to be the cries of the Ahool itself.

The audio recordings reveal a cacophony of sounds, echoing through the dense undergrowth. The piercing screeches, a chilling combination of gibbon-like howls and bat-like screeches, send shivers down the spine of anyone who listens. The recordings, although unsettling, serve as a testament to the presence of an unidentified and highly vocal creature within these rainforest realms.

Furthermore, the tales and audio recordings are not isolated incidents. They are part of a larger tapestry of cryptid lore that has persisted for centuries. Indigenous tribes, with their deep connection to the land and its creatures, have contributed to the rich tapestry of legends surrounding the Ahool. Their oral traditions and stories serve as a testament to the creature's existence and continue to foster intrigue and fascination among those who delve into the realm of cryptids.

As researchers and enthusiasts continue to explore the rainforests of Java and Sumatra, the Ahool remains an enigma, an elusive entity that defies easy classification. The legends, eyewitness accounts, and audio recordings all contribute to the mounting evidence that there is something extraordinary lurking within these dense jungles.

The Ahool's presence in the collective consciousness of the region persists, tantalising and urging further investigation. The allure of its mystique and the desire to unravel its secrets will continue to fuel expeditions, scientific inquiries, and the imaginations of those drawn to the captivating world of cryptozoology.

Scientific Possibilities and Alternative Explanations

WHILE THE LEGENDS, eyewitness accounts, and audio recordings associated with the Ahool paint a compelling picture of a bat-like creature dwelling in the rainforests of Java and Sumatra, it is essential to explore the scientific possibilities and alternative explanations that may shed light on these reported sightings.

Misidentified Known Species

ONE PLAUSIBLE EXPLANATION for Ahool sightings is the misidentification of known bat species. Bats are incredibly diverse, and their appearances can vary significantly. It is possible that witnesses encountered a large, uncommon species of bat that exhibits ape-like features due to lighting conditions, perspective, or fear-induced exaggeration.

Hoaxes and Misinterpretations

CRYPTID SIGHTINGS ARE sometimes the result of hoaxes or misinterpretations of natural phenomena. In the case of the Ahool, it is conceivable that some sightings were fabricated or exaggerated for various reasons, such as seeking attention or perpetuating local folklore. Misidentifications of large birds or other animals, coupled with an atmosphere of mystery and imagination, may have contributed to the creation of Ahool legends.

Psychological and Perceptual Factors

HUMAN PERCEPTION CAN be influenced by psychological factors, including expectation bias and suggestibility. The power of suggestion or cultural beliefs may shape witnesses' perceptions, leading them to interpret ordinary animal sightings as encounters with the Ahool. Additionally, the dark and dense rainforest environment can play tricks on the mind, creating illusions and heightened emotions that contribute to the creation of supernatural narratives.

Unknown Species or Cryptid

ALTHOUGH THE EXISTENCE of the Ahool remains unproven, the rainforests of Java and Sumatra are home to a vast array of undiscovered species. It is plausible that the Ahool could be a unique and as yet undocumented creature, potentially a new species of bat or primate that has adapted to its rainforest habitat. Further scientific exploration and thorough field investigations are necessary to substantiate this possibility.

Cultural Significance and Symbolism

THE AHOOL'S PRESENCE in local folklore and cultural traditions cannot be ignored. Cryptids often serve as symbols that represent deeper cultural or environmental concerns. The Ahool might embody the awe-inspiring power of nature, the mysteries of the rainforest, or the delicate balance between human beings and the natural world. Viewing the Ahool from this perspective allows us to appreciate its significance beyond its literal existence or non-existence.

As with any cryptid, the School's existence remains elusive, and scientific investigation plays a crucial role in uncovering the truth. Cryptozoologists, biologists, and explorers continue to explore the rainforests, employing advanced techniques like camera traps, DNA analysis, and acoustic monitoring to gather evidence. Through rigorous scientific inquiry, the Ahool's enigma may ultimately be deciphered.

While scepticism is essential in evaluating cryptid sightings, it is equally important to approach these investigations with an open mind. The possibility of discovering a new species or gaining a deeper understanding of the natural world adds excitement and wonder to scientific endeavours. The Ahool, with its captivating tales and mysterious allure, serves as a reminder that our planet still holds countless secrets, waiting patiently to be uncovered and understood.

The Cultural Significance of the Ahool

THE AHOOL, WITH ITS enigmatic presence and mysterious allure, extends beyond mere cryptozoology to become deeply intertwined with the cultural fabric of the regions it is said to inhabit. Within the rich tapestry of local folklore and mythological narratives, the Ahool assumes a symbolic significance that extends far beyond its reported sightings.

Nature's Majesty and Mystery

THE AHOOL'S ASSOCIATION with the rainforests of Java and Sumatra elevates its status to that of a guardian or embodiment of the natural world. Within indigenous cultures, the rainforest is often regarded as a sacred realm, home to ancestral spirits and unseen forces. The Ahool, with its eerie cries and elusive nature, becomes a representative of the awe-inspiring power and impenetrable mysteries that lie within the heart of the rainforest.

Balance between Humanity and Nature

CRYPTIDS LIKE THE AHOOL often serve as reminders of the delicate equilibrium between human beings and the natural world. These creatures embody the need for harmony and respect between humans and their environment. The Ahool's presence within local folklore underscores the importance of preserving the rainforest and its inhabitants, fostering a deeper connection with the natural world and a recognition of our place within it.

Lessons of Fear and Respect

THE SCHOOL'S REPUTATION as a formidable and fearsome creature also carries valuable lessons. Legends and stories associated with the Ahool warn against venturing too far into the rainforest without proper reverence and caution. The creature's chilling cries and mysterious presence instil a sense of awe and respect for the untamed wilderness, encouraging a mindful approach to engaging with nature's secrets.

The Power of Myth and Imagination

THE SCHOOL'S EXISTENCE, or lack thereof, within local mythological narratives speaks to the power of collective imagination and storytelling. Legends of the Ahool captivate the minds of communities, instilling a sense of wonder and enchantment. These tales are passed down through generations, connecting individuals to their cultural heritage and fostering a shared sense of identity rooted in the land and its mysteries.

Cultural Identity and Heritage

THE AHOOL'S PRESENCE in local folklore adds to the cultural identity and heritage of the communities that believe in its existence. It becomes a source of pride, a symbol of their unique connection to the natural world and the narratives that have shaped their history. The Ahool represents the resilience and adaptability of these cultures, as their stories continue to endure, bridging the gap between past and present.

In exploring the cultural significance of the Ahool, we find that it transcends the realm of a mere cryptid. It becomes a vessel through which deeper connections are formed between humanity and nature, between generations, and between individual and collective imagination. The Ahool's place within broader mythological narratives reminds us of the enduring power of stories and their ability to shape our understanding of the world around us.

Whether the Ahool is a product of folklore, misidentification, or an undiscovered species, its cultural significance remains undiminished. The stories and beliefs associated with the Ahool continue to captivate, inspire, and foster a sense of wonder that extends far beyond the realm of the tangible. In this way, the Ahool transcends its cryptid status, becoming a symbol of the profound connections between humanity, nature, and the power of storytelling.

Chapter 8: The Enigma of the Yowie

The vast continent of Australia is home to a myriad of captivating creatures, both real and mythical. Among the most intriguing is the legendary Yowie, a cryptid that has fascinated both locals and cryptozoologists alike. While primarily known in Australia, there have been sporadic reports of Yowie sightings in Southeast Asia, adding to the mystique surrounding this enigmatic creature. In this chapter, we delve into the origins and cultural significance of the Yowie, unravelling the legends and stories that have woven its existence into the fabric of the land.

Origins and Folklore

THE YOWIE, ALSO KNOWN as the Australian Bigfoot, is deeply entrenched in the Aboriginal lore and oral traditions. The ancient tales passed down through generations depict the Yowie as a towering, hairy creature, akin to the Yeti of the Himalayas or Sasquatch of North America. However, unlike its counterparts, the Yowie is said to possess a distinctively apelike appearance, often described as possessing a muscular build, long arms, and a protruding forehead.

Aboriginal cultures across Australia have different names for the Yowie, reflecting the rich diversity of the indigenous peoples. In the Bundjalung culture, it is referred to as the "Tarrawarra," a powerful spirit believed to inhabit the dense forests and rugged mountain ranges. In the Yowie-obsessed region of Queensland, the creature is known as "Quinkin" or "Jingera," often depicted in rock art and cave paintings, further testament to its cultural significance.

Cultural Significance

TO THE ABORIGINAL COMMUNITIES, the Yowie is much more than just a mythical creature; it is a guardian of the land, embodying the connection between the natural world and the spiritual realm. In their belief system, the Yowie is seen as a powerful and sometimes mischievous being, possessing the ability to shape-shift and move swiftly between the human and animal realms. It is revered as a symbol of both fear and respect, cautioning those who trespass on sacred lands.

The Yowie's cultural significance extends beyond the Aboriginal communities. In contemporary Australian culture, the Yowie has become a beloved figure, inspiring numerous stories, books, and even a popular line of chocolate treats. It has become an emblem of the country's fascination with the mysterious and unknown, a reminder that the vast Australian wilderness still harbours secrets waiting to be discovered.

Southeast Asian Connections

WHILE THE YOWIE IS primarily associated with the Australian continent, intriguingly, there have been reported sightings of similar hairy hominid creatures in parts of Southeast Asia. These sightings have piqued the curiosity of cryptozoologists, who speculate on the possibility of a shared origin or a migration of these cryptids across land bridges that once connected the continents.

In the dense rainforests of Indonesia, locals speak of a creature known as the "Orang Pendek," which bears a striking resemblance to the Yowie. Descriptions of the Orang Pendek align with the Yowie's physical attributes, suggesting a possible connection between these elusive beings. These reported sightings, though scattered and anecdotal, hint at the interconnectedness of cryptid legends across the region.

The Yowie stands as a testament to the enduring power of folklore and the human fascination with the unknown. Rooted in the rich tapestry of Aboriginal culture, this towering figure has become an iconic symbol of Australia's wilderness and its untamed mysteries. The reported sightings in Southeast Asia add an intriguing layer to the Yowie's story, hinting at the possibility of a shared ancestry and bridging the gaps between distant lands.

Whether regarded as a guardian, a creature of myth, or an elusive being of the wild, the Yowie continues to capture the imagination of those who seek to uncover the truth behind its existence. It serves as a reminder that amidst the modern world, there are still enigmatic creatures lurking in the depths of unexplored territories.

As the stories and legends of the Yowie persist, researchers and enthusiasts venture into the rugged Australian outback and the dense forests of Southeast Asia, armed with cameras, recording devices, and an insatiable curiosity. Their quest is not only to catch a glimpse of the Yowie but also to shed light on the mysteries that surround it.

While scientific evidence remains scarce, the cultural significance of the Yowie cannot be denied. It serves as a bridge between the Aboriginal heritage and the contemporary fascination with cryptozoology. The Yowie's legacy endures in the tales shared around campfires, the artwork adorning cave walls, and the whispered encounters passed down through generations.

Whether the Yowie exists as a flesh-and-blood creature or exists solely within the realm of myth and legend, its impact on the cultural landscape is undeniable. It embodies the spirit of the untamed wilderness, reminding us that there are still secrets waiting to be unravelled, and that the world is full of wonders yet to be discovered.

As the sun sets over the vast Australian outback, casting long shadows across the rugged terrain, the mystery of the Yowie lives on. It continues to capture the hearts and minds of those who dare to believe in the extraordinary, and beckons us to explore the unexplored, for it is in the pursuit of the unknown that we truly understand the depth of our connection to the world around us.

And so, the Yowie remains an enigma, a creature of whispers and sightings, an embodiment of the wild and the unknown, forever woven into the tapestry of Australian folklore and beyond. Its presence lingers in the shadows, reminding us that there is still much more to learn about the vast and diverse cryptid realm that stretches across the captivating landscapes of Asia.

Descriptions, Behaviours, and Habitats of the Yowie Across Different Regions

THE YOWIE, KNOWN AS the Australian Bigfoot, is a cryptid that has captured the imagination of people across the vast and diverse continent of Australia. While primarily associated with the Australian outback, reports and sightings of similar creatures have also emerged from various regions in Southeast Asia. Although the descriptions, behaviours, and habitats of the Yowie may vary slightly across different locations, certain commonalities can be found.

The Yowie is commonly described as a large, ape-like creature standing anywhere from 6 to 10 feet tall. It is said to have a robust, muscular build, covered in shaggy, coarse hair that ranges in colour from reddish-brown to dark brown or black. Witnesses often note its distinctively apelike features, including a prominent forehead, deep-set eyes, and a wide, flat nose. The Yowie is said to possess long arms that hang down past its knees, and its footprint is often described as large and elongated, resembling that of a human foot but with a broader shape.

The behaviour of the Yowie is largely characterised by its elusive nature. It is commonly reported to be a shy and reclusive creature, preferring to avoid human contact and retreat into remote, secluded areas. Witnesses often describe the Yowie as moving with great stealth and agility, capable of disappearing into the dense vegetation of the Australian bush or the Southeast Asian rainforests with remarkable ease. Some accounts suggest that the Yowie possesses a curious and inquisitive nature, observing humans from a distance but swiftly retreating when detected.

There have been occasional reports of aggressive behaviour attributed to the Yowie, particularly when it feels threatened or cornered. These incidents typically involve displays of intimidation, such as loud vocalisations, tree shaking, or throwing rocks. However, direct physical attacks are rare, and the Yowie is not generally considered to be a danger to humans.

The Yowie is commonly associated with remote and rugged habitats, where it can find ample cover and seclusion. In Australia, it is often linked to the expansive outback, with its vast stretches of arid deserts, rocky mountain ranges, and dense scrubland. The Yowie is said to thrive in these harsh and unforgiving environments, utilising caves, dense vegetation, and natural rock formations as shelters.

In Southeast Asia, reports of similar creatures often emerge from the lush rainforests and jungles that blanket the region. These habitats provide abundant food sources, including fruits, nuts, and small animals, allowing the Yowie to sustain itself. It is believed to navigate the dense foliage and rugged terrain with ease, relying on its strength and agility to move swiftly and remain hidden from prying eyes.

It is important to note that the specific habitats of the Yowie can vary depending on the region and local geography.

Sightings have been reported near water sources such as rivers and lakes, suggesting that the Yowie may have an affinity for these areas as well.

While the descriptions, behaviours, and habitats of the Yowie may exhibit some variation across different regions, certain commonalities persist. The Yowie is often described as a large, ape-like creature, reclusive in nature, and inhabiting remote and rugged environments. As sightings and reports continue to emerge, further exploration and investigation into the mysterious world of the Yowie may shed more light on its true nature and existence.

Unravelling the true nature of the Yowie remains a challenge. With the advancements in technology and increased interest in cryptozoology, researchers are employing various methods to gather evidence, including footprint analysis, DNA testing, and the use of remote sensing techniques. These efforts aim to unravel the mysteries surrounding the Yowie, its origins, and its place within the ecosystem.

As our understanding of the Yowie evolves, it becomes evident that this cryptid holds a significant place in the cultural heritage and natural mythology of the regions it inhabits. It continues to capture the fascination of those who seek to uncover its existence, reminding us that there are still untamed corners of the world where creatures of mystery dwell, waiting to be discovered.

EDWARD TURNER

Chapter Nine: The Chupacabra of the Philippines

The Chupacabra is a cryptid that has been reported throughout the Americas, but few people know that there have been sightings of the creature in the Philippines as well. The Chupacabra, meaning "goat sucker" in Spanish, has been described as a creature with spines or quills running down its back, long claws, and a tendency to attack and kill livestock.

The first reported sighting of the Chupacabra in the Philippines was in the early 2000s, when farmers began to report the strange deaths of their livestock. The animals were found with puncture wounds on their necks, and their blood drained from their bodies. Local villagers reported seeing a strange creature lurking around the farms at night, but the description of the creature did not match any known animals in the area.

The Chupacabra sightings in the Philippines were initially dismissed as hoaxes or exaggerations, but as more and more farmers reported missing livestock, the local authorities began to take the sightings seriously. The creatures were described as having a reptilian appearance, with scales and leathery skin, and long, sharp claws.

Interestingly, the Chupacabra sightings in the Philippines bear a striking resemblance to the better-known legend of the Chupacabra in Latin America. The Latin American

Chupacabra is said to be a creature that attacks and kills livestock, draining their blood and leaving behind puncture wounds on their necks. The creature is also described as having a reptilian appearance, with spines running down its back and large, sharp claws.

The similarities between the two legends have led some researchers to suggest that the Chupacabra sightings in the Philippines may be connected to the Latin American legend. It is possible that the creature migrated from Latin America to the Philippines, either through natural means or by human intervention.

There are also those who believe that the Chupacabra is a creature that has always existed in different parts of the world, but has only recently come to the attention of humans due to increased media attention and awareness. Whatever the case may be, the Chupacabra remains a mysterious and elusive cryptid, with sightings reported around the world. Whether it is a real creature or simply a legend remains to be seen, but for the farmers in the Philippines who have lost their livestock to this creature, the Chupacabra is all too real.

Eyewitness Testimonies

AS THE REPORTS OF CHUPACABRA sightings in the Philippines multiplied, so did the number of eyewitness testimonies. Farmers, who were the first to encounter the creature, described it with a mixture of fear and disbelief. Many claimed to have seen a strange, reptilian creature lurking near their farms during the late hours of the night.

One farmer, Juanito Reyes, recounted his encounter with the Chupacabra. He had gone out to check on his goats one moonlit night when he saw a shadowy figure moving quickly among the herd. As he approached, he noticed the creature's glowing eyes and its bizarre features. Reyes described it as having scaly skin, a hunched back with spines, and long, menacing claws.

Similar descriptions were given by other eyewitnesses, painting a consistent picture of the Chupacabra's appearance. Their accounts spoke of a creature that seemed to blend elements of reptiles and otherworldly beings. These testimonies provided a chilling reminder of the mysterious nature of this cryptid.

Livestock Attacks

THE CHUPACABRA'S EMERGENCE in the Philippines was accompanied by a disturbing wave of livestock attacks. Farmers woke up to a grisly sight, finding their animals dead with peculiar wounds on their necks. The victims included not only goats but also chickens, pigs, and even larger animals such as cows and carabaos.

What perplexed the farmers was the manner in which the animals were killed. The wounds appeared to be clean puncture marks, as if something had deliberately drained their blood. Many carcasses were found completely devoid of this vital fluid, leading to speculation about the creature's insidious feeding habits.

The Mysterious Blood-Draining

Phenomena

THE MOST PERPLEXING aspect of the Chupacabra phenomenon was the way it seemed to drain the blood from its victims. Unlike typical predator attacks, where bloodstains and scattered remains were left behind, the Chupacabra left behind a macabre scene. Livestock carcasses were found with no signs of external trauma other than the puncture wounds on their necks. Yet, these wounds were precise, suggesting a calculated method of blood extraction.

Scientists and experts struggled to explain this mysterious blood-draining phenomenon. Some proposed that the creature possessed specialised fangs or appendages, capable of piercing the skin without causing extensive damage. Others speculated that the Chupacabra had a unique method of blood consumption, perhaps utilising a proboscis or an elongated tongue.

Despite investigations and numerous theories, the exact mechanism behind the blood-draining phenomenon remained elusive. The phenomenon itself added an eerie and unsettling layer to the already chilling encounters with the Chupacabra.

The emergence of the Chupacabra in the Philippines, with its eyewitness testimonies, livestock attacks, and mysterious blood-draining phenomena, intensified the mystery surrounding this cryptid. The people who lived in the affected areas found themselves caught between disbelief and terror, struggling to comprehend the existence of such a creature. The investigation into the Chupacabra would continue, as researchers sought answers to its origin, behaviour, and the ominous phenomenon surrounding its attacks.

Theories Surrounding the Origin and Nature of the Chupacabra

THE CHUPACABRA'S EXISTENCE remains a mystery to this day, and many theories have been put forward to explain its origin and nature. While some believe that the Chupacabra is a real creature that has yet to be discovered, others argue that it is a myth or a product of collective hysteria. Here are some of the most popular theories surrounding the Chupacabra:

Theory 1: Extraterrestrial

ONE THEORY POSITS THAT the Chupacabra is a creature from outer space. Supporters of this theory point to the creature's unusual appearance and bizarre behaviour, which suggest that it is not of this world. They also argue that the Chupacabra's emergence in different parts of the world indicates that it may be an alien species that is adapting to various environments.

Theory 2: Genetic Experiment

ANOTHER THEORY SUGGESTS that the Chupacabra is a result of a genetic experiment gone awry. Supporters of this theory argue that the creature's appearance and behaviour indicate that it is a product of genetic modification, possibly conducted in a laboratory. This theory gained traction in the

1990s when some claimed that the Chupacabra was a government experiment gone wrong.

Theory 3: Cryptid

THE CHUPACABRA IS OFTEN classified as a cryptid, which means that it is an animal whose existence has not been scientifically proven. Some believe that the Chupacabra is a real creature, albeit an elusive one. They argue that the creature's appearance and behaviour are consistent with that of other cryptids, such as Bigfoot and the Loch Ness Monster.

Theory 4: Myth

SCEPTICS ARGUE THAT the Chupacabra is nothing more than a myth. They claim that the creature's existence is based on hearsay and rumours, and that there is no concrete evidence to support its existence. They argue that the Chupacabra is a product of collective hysteria, fueled by media sensationalism and the desire for attention.

The origin and nature of the Chupacabra continue to be shrouded in mystery, and there is no consensus on what it really is. While some believe that it is a real creature, others argue that it is a product of imagination or a scientific experiment gone awry. The investigation into the Chupacabra will likely continue, and perhaps one day we will have a definitive answer to this enigmatic cryptid.

Cultural Implications and Local Beliefs

THE EMERGENCE OF THE Chupacabra in the Philippines brought forth various cultural implications and local beliefs surrounding this cryptid. Folklore and traditional beliefs intertwined with the encounters, shaping the perceptions and reactions of the communities affected by the Chupacabra phenomenon.

Folklore and Mythology

IN THE PHILIPPINES, a country rich in folklore and mythical creatures, the Chupacabra quickly found its place among the pantheon of supernatural beings. Local legends and tales of shape-shifting creatures and blood-sucking monsters provided a backdrop for interpreting the Chupacabra sightings. Some communities saw it as a manifestation of ancient folklore come to life, while others saw it as a new addition to the local mythology.

Superstitions and Omens

THE ARRIVAL OF THE Chupacabra was also accompanied by a host of superstitions and beliefs. Some villagers believed that sighting the Chupacabra was an omen of impending misfortune or tragedy. Others viewed it as a sign of supernatural disturbance in the area, prompting rituals and offerings to appease the creature and protect the community from its wrath.

Fear and Panic

THE PRESENCE OF THE Chupacabra instilled fear and panic among the affected communities. The mystery surrounding its nature and potential danger fueled rumours and exaggerated stories, further heightening anxiety. Farmers became increasingly concerned for their livestock, taking extra precautions to safeguard them from the alleged predator. The fear of the Chupacabra permeated daily life, altering routines and provoking a sense of vulnerability.

Cultural Resilience and Adaptation

AS WITH ANY CULTURAL phenomenon, communities responded in their own unique ways. Some turned to their traditional practices and rituals, seeking solace and protection from the Chupacabra. Others relied on modern technology and scientific investigations, hoping to find logical explanations for the sightings. The local culture displayed resilience in the face of uncertainty, adapting to the challenges posed by the presence of this cryptid.

Tourism and Popular Culture

THE CHUPACABRA SIGHTINGS in the Philippines also had an impact on tourism and popular culture. The allure of encountering such a mysterious creature attracted curious visitors and enthusiasts. Local businesses capitalised on the Chupacabra phenomenon, offering guided tours and merchandise related to the cryptid. Books, movies, and television shows incorporated the Chupacabra into their narratives, further perpetuating its presence in popular culture.

The emergence of the Chupacabra in the Philippines had profound cultural implications and triggered a range of local beliefs. It merged with existing folklore, fueled superstitions, and provoked fear and panic. However, communities also displayed resilience and adapted to the presence of this cryptid, incorporating it into their cultural fabric. The Chupacabra's impact extended beyond local communities, influencing tourism and popular culture, and ensuring its enduring place in the cultural tapestry of the Philippines.

Chapter 10: Tsuchinoko

The sun dipped below the horizon, casting long shadows across the dense forest of Mount Fuji. Amidst the ancient trees and mysterious mist, a creature lurked—a creature steeped in the folklore and legends of Japan. Known as the Tsuchinoko, this enigmatic serpent has captured the imaginations of countless generations with its peculiar appearance and elusive nature.

The tales of the Tsuchinoko trace back centuries, whispered around campfires and shared among villagers. In Japanese mythology, it is often depicted as a snake-like creature, about one metre long, with a thick, bulbous body and a head that resembles a mix of a snake and a lizard. Its most distinctive feature is its ability to move in a sidewinding motion, enabling it to traverse even the steepest of terrains with ease.

Legends abound regarding the Tsuchinoko's behaviour and abilities. It is believed to possess venomous fangs, capable of delivering a deadly bite. However, some accounts tell a different story, portraying the creature as benign and even helpful, possessing supernatural powers of healing and good fortune.

In rural areas of Japan, encounters with the Tsuchinoko are whispered about with equal parts excitement and trepidation. Locals claim that the creature emits a distinct chirping or squeaking sound, which has earned it the nickname "barking snake" due to its resemblance to a dog's bark. These vocalisations add an eerie quality to the stories, as if the Tsuchinoko is communicating with those who dare to venture into its domain.

Yet, despite the tales and occasional sightings, the Tsuchinoko remains a creature of mystery. It has proven remarkably adept at evading capture, leading many to wonder if it possesses supernatural powers of invisibility or shape-shifting. Its ability to camouflage itself in its surroundings further complicates the task of those who seek to unravel its secrets.

As with many cryptids, the Tsuchinoko has its fair share of sceptics who dismiss it as nothing more than a product of folklore and exaggeration. They attribute reported sightings to misidentified snakes or clever hoaxes. However, for those who have experienced the Tsuchinoko firsthand, there is an unshakeable belief that something truly extraordinary dwells within the depths of Japan's wilderness.

Efforts to document and study the Tsuchinoko have been met with numerous challenges. Its elusive nature and preference for remote locations make it a difficult subject to observe and study scientifically. Nonetheless, cryptozoologists and enthusiasts persist in their quest to shed light on this captivating creature. Expeditions are organised, employing cutting-edge technology and traditional tracking methods, yet the Tsuchinoko remains one step ahead, leaving behind only fleeting traces of its presence.

Perhaps the Tsuchinoko is more than a physical entity. It exists as a bridge between the tangible and the intangible, embodying the rich tapestry of Japan's folklore and cultural heritage. It serves as a reminder that even in the modern world, there are mysteries yet to be unravelled, secrets yet to be unveiled.

So, the Tsuchinoko continues to captivate the hearts and minds of those who seek to understand the enigma that lies within its serpentine form. As the moon rises over the mountains and darkness shrouds the land, the legend of the Tsuchinoko lives on—a testament to the enduring power of myth and the allure of the unknown.

And as long as the forests of Japan whisper their secrets, the Tsuchinoko will remain an enigmatic figure, forever entwined with the fabric of the country's folklore, waiting for the next curious soul to venture into its realm and catch a glimpse of its mysterious existence in the hopes of unravelling the truth behind its existence. Tsuchinoko is more than just a creature of myth and legend—it represents the spirit of exploration, curiosity, and the deep connection between humans and nature.

As the years pass and technology advances, the search for the Tsuchinoko will continue. It may take a breakthrough in scientific methodology or a chance encounter by an intrepid explorer to finally bring this elusive cryptid into the realm of verifiable evidence. Until then, the Tsuchinoko will persist as a symbol of the unknown and a reminder that there are still mysteries in the world waiting to be discovered.

So, if you ever find yourself wandering through the ancient forests of Japan, listen closely to the whispers of the wind and the rustling of leaves. Keep your senses alert, for the Tsuchinoko may be watching, slithering through the undergrowth with its keen eyes and quick wit. And if you're fortunate enough to catch a glimpse of this legendary creature, cherish the moment, for you will become part of a tale passed down through generations—a witness to the magic and wonder that dwells within the heart of Japanese folklore.

The Tsuchinoko, with its mysterious allure, will forever inspire a sense of adventure and ignite the imagination of those who dare to believe. For in a world where science and reality often govern our perceptions, the cryptids that inhabit our folklore and mythology serve as a reminder that there are still secrets waiting to be uncovered, reminding us to embrace the unknown and embrace the mysteries that lie just beyond our reach.

Varied Descriptions and Regional Variations

THROUGHOUT THE FOLKLORE and legends of Japan, the Tsuchinoko has been depicted in various forms, with its appearance and characteristics often varying from region to region. This chapter delves into the intriguing diversity of descriptions and regional variations surrounding this enigmatic serpent.

In the central regions of Japan, particularly in areas around Mount Fuji and the Kanto region, the Tsuchinoko is commonly described as a snake-like creature with a plump body, resembling a stubby sausage or a beer bottle. It is said to have a head that is distinctively wider than its neck, giving it a distinctive appearance. Some accounts even mention small, claw-like appendages or short, stumpy legs, though such features are not universally reported.

Venturing towards western Japan, the Tsuchinoko takes on a slightly different form. Here, it is often depicted with a long, slender body and a head resembling that of a viper or a dragon. The snake-like nature of the creature remains consistent, but its overall shape and proportions vary, highlighting the richness of the creature's folklore across different regions.

In the northernmost reaches of Japan, where the winters are harsh and the landscapes are rugged, the Tsuchinoko is said to possess adaptations suited to its environment. It is described as having a thick, insulating layer of fur or scales that help it withstand the cold. This regional variation reflects the adaptability and resourcefulness attributed to the Tsuchinoko, enabling it to thrive in diverse habitats across the country.

Another intriguing aspect of the Tsuchinoko's regional variations lies in its reported behaviours and abilities. In some areas, it is considered a shy and reclusive creature, often avoiding human contact and swiftly disappearing into the underbrush at the first sign of danger. However, in other regions, it is believed to possess mischievous or even malevolent traits, with tales of the Tsuchinoko causing crop failures or bringing bad luck to those who encounter it.

Furthermore, the Tsuchinoko's vocalisations also exhibit regional diversity. In the southern regions of Japan, its chirping or squeaking sound is described as high-pitched and melodic, often likened to the song of a bird. In contrast, in the mountainous areas, the Tsuchinoko's vocalisations take on a deeper, resonating tone, akin to the growl of a wild beast. These variations in sound add another layer of intrigue and mystery to the creature's folklore, captivating the imagination of those who hear the tales.

The varied descriptions and regional variations of the Tsuchinoko highlight the rich tapestry of Japan's folklore and cultural diversity. They demonstrate how different communities interpret and shape the legends of this mythical serpent, integrating it into their local traditions and beliefs. These variations also emphasise the adaptability of folklore, as it evolves and takes on new characteristics depending on the environment and the people who pass down the stories.

Whether the Tsuchinoko is a physical entity that roams the forests and mountains of Japan or an embodiment of the collective imagination, one thing remains clear—it has captured the hearts and minds of the Japanese people for centuries. The diverse descriptions and regional variations only add to its allure, making the Tsuchinoko a truly captivating and enduring figure in the cryptid lore of Asia.

Sightings, Encounters, and Cultural Beliefs

THE TSUCHINOKO, WITH its mythical presence and elusive nature, has left an indelible mark on the cultural beliefs and traditions of Japan. Tales of sightings and encounters with this enigmatic creature have been passed down through generations, captivating the imagination of the people and weaving it into the fabric of their folklore. This chapter explores the intriguing world of Tsuchinoko sightings, encounters, and the cultural beliefs surrounding this elusive cryptid.

Stories of Tsuchinoko sightings can be traced back for centuries, spanning different regions of Japan. These accounts often share common elements, describing a snake-like creature with a thick, bulbous body and distinct head. However, the details and circumstances surrounding the encounters vary, adding layers of intrigue to Tsuchinoko's mystique.

In some instances, locals claim to have stumbled upon a Tsuchinoko while tending to their daily tasks. Farmers working in the fields recount moments when they spotted the creature slithering through the grass or hiding amidst the crops. These encounters are often brief and fleeting, leaving witnesses awestruck and questioning the reality of what they witnessed.

Other sightings occur during expeditions into the deep forests and mountainous regions. Hikers and explorers report unexpected encounters with the Tsuchinoko, describing its sidewinding movement and unique features. Such encounters tend to evoke a mix of fascination, curiosity, and even a sense of reverence for the creature.

However, it is important to acknowledge that scepticism exists surrounding the authenticity of these sightings. Critics argue that misidentified snakes, hoaxes, or the blending of imagination and reality might contribute to the reports. Yet, despite the scepticism, the belief in the Tsuchinoko remains steadfast among those who claim to have witnessed its presence.

Cultural beliefs surrounding the Tsuchinoko further illustrate its significance within Japanese folklore. In some regions, the creature is revered as a guardian of the natural world, embodying the spirit of nature itself. It is believed to possess supernatural powers, such as healing abilities or the capacity to bring good fortune to those who encounter it with respect and reverence.

Conversely, in certain communities, the Tsuchinoko is regarded with caution or fear. Its association with crop failures, bad luck, or even acts of vengeance adds a darker undertone to the creature's mythos. It is said that disturbing or harming a Tsuchinoko can bring about misfortune or disaster upon the offender and their community.

The cultural significance of the Tsuchinoko is also reflected in various festivals and rituals throughout Japan. In some regions, festivals are held to honour and celebrate the creature, with processions, dances, and offerings made in its name. These traditions demonstrate the enduring impact the Tsuchinoko has had on local communities and their collective identity.

In modern times, the fascination with the Tsuchinoko has not waned. Cryptid enthusiasts, researchers, and adventurers embark on expeditions, armed with cameras and scientific equipment, in the hopes of capturing definitive evidence of its existence. Expeditions are conducted, diligently searching for clues, tracks, or any physical proof that could validate the tales and legends that have persisted for centuries.

Whether the Tsuchinoko is a tangible creature dwelling in the depths of Japan's wilderness or an ethereal being that embodies the spirit of nature itself, its influence on Japanese culture and belief systems cannot be denied. It continues to captivate the hearts and minds of the people, reminding them of the mysterious wonders that lie just beyond their grasp.

As the Tsuchinoko remains elusive, sightings and encounters become fragments of a grand tapestry that weaves together the traditions, beliefs, and folklore of Japan. The allure of the Tsuchinoko lies not only in the quest for evidence but also in the intangible realm of wonder and imagination.

The Tsuchinoko serves as a reminder of the intrinsic human fascination with the unknown and the enduring power of myth and folklore. It embodies the delicate balance between the tangible and the intangible, the seen and the unseen. Its presence in the cultural landscape of Japan is a testament to the profound connection between humans and the natural world.

As the years pass and the modern world progresses, the mystery of the Tsuchinoko continues to beckon curious souls. It is a call to explore, to embrace the enigmatic, and to recognize that amidst the concrete jungles and technological marvels, there are still uncharted territories waiting to be discovered.

Whether the Tsuchinoko exists as a physical entity or resides solely within the realm of human imagination, its legacy endures. It serves as a symbol of the rich tapestry of Japanese folklore, inspiring awe, curiosity, and a deep appreciation for the wonders that lie beyond the boundaries of what we know.

So, let us keep the spirit of the Tsuchinoko alive within us, nurturing a sense of wonder and embracing the mysteries that surround us. For it is in the pursuit of these mysteries that we embark on a journey of discovery, connecting with the ancient stories and beliefs that shape our collective consciousness.

And perhaps, one day, the elusive Tsuchinoko will reveal itself, stepping out of the realms of myth and into the realm of undeniable truth. Until then, it remains an enigma—an enigmatic serpent that slithers through the landscape of Japanese folklore, reminding us to cherish the mysteries that lie within our world and within ourselves.

Scientific Explanations and the Influence of Folklore

THE TSUCHINOKO, WITH its mythical presence and elusive nature, has long intrigued both believers and sceptics alike. While sightings and encounters have been reported throughout history, scientific explanations attempt to shed light on the mysterious creature. Additionally, the role of folklore in shaping the perception of the Tsuchinoko cannot be overlooked. This chapter explores the potential scientific explanations for Tsuchinoko sightings and the influence of folklore on its perception.

One scientific explanation for Tsuchinoko sightings revolves around misidentification. It is plausible that encounters with ordinary snake species could be mistaken for the Tsuchinoko due to environmental factors or human error. Different snake species, such as the Japanese rat snake or the Japanese keelback, share certain physical characteristics with the Tsuchinoko, leading to confusion in identification. The human mind, influenced by the legends and descriptions of the Tsuchinoko, may inadvertently impose these features onto observed snakes, creating the illusion of encountering the cryptid.

Another scientific consideration is the presence of hoaxes and exaggerations. Folklore and legends surrounding the Tsuchinoko have built up expectations and beliefs over time, making it susceptible to hoaxes and fabricated accounts. In some instances, individuals seeking attention or perpetuating the mystery may create elaborate stories or even construct fake Tsuchinoko specimens, contributing to the complexity of distinguishing genuine encounters from fictional ones.

Moreover, psychological factors play a significant role in the perception and interpretation of Tsuchinoko sightings. The power of suggestion and cultural beliefs can shape how individuals perceive and recall their experiences. When people are primed with the notion of encountering a Tsuchinoko, their minds may interpret ordinary events or encounters with snakes as evidence of the cryptid's existence. This cognitive bias can influence the recollection and retelling of stories, further blurring the line between fact and fiction.

However, it is essential to recognize that scientific explanations do not discount the cultural significance and impact of folklore on the perception of the Tsuchinoko. Folklore plays a vital role in shaping how individuals interpret and understand the world around them. It serves as a framework through which people make sense of their experiences, creating a sense of identity, community, and shared beliefs.

The Tsuchinoko's presence in Japanese folklore serves as a cultural touchstone, connecting people to their heritage and the natural world. Its inclusion in traditional tales, rituals, and festivals underscores the deep reverence and respect for nature that permeates Japanese culture. The stories and beliefs surrounding the Tsuchinoko reflect the human fascination with the unknown, the exploration of the natural world, and the preservation of traditions.

In this context, folklore and scientific explanations are not mutually exclusive. The Tsuchinoko can exist as both a creature of myth and a subject of scientific inquiry. The interplay between these realms fosters a sense of wonder and curiosity, encouraging individuals to explore the boundaries between belief and knowledge.

ASIA'S TOP TEN CRYPTIDS: LEGENDS, SIGHTINGS, AND THEORIES

As we unravel the scientific explanations behind Tsuchinoko sightings, it is crucial to preserve and respect the cultural significance of this legendary creature. The Tsuchinoko's influence on folklore and its enduring presence within Japanese society highlight the profound connection between humans, nature, and the stories we tell.

Ultimately, the enigma of the Tsuchinoko serves as a reminder that the mysteries of the world are not solely scientific puzzles to be solved but also tales to be cherished and shared. By embracing both the scientific and cultural dimensions of the Tsuchinoko, we can embark on a journey of discovery, exploring the realms of possibility and imagination that enrich our understanding of the natural world and ourselves.

EDWARD TURNER

The End of the Journey

As we come to the end of this remarkable journey through the fascinating realm of Asia's cryptid lore, it is only fitting to reflect on the incredible exploration we have undertaken, delving into the mysteries of ten captivating creatures that have intrigued and bewildered generations.

From the dense jungles of Southeast Asia to the soaring peaks of the Himalayas and the ancient forests of Japan, we have traversed vast landscapes, delving deep into the heart of legends and myths to uncover the truth behind these elusive beings.

Our expedition began with the awe-inspiring majesty of the Yeti, a legendary creature shrouded in icy enigma. We followed its elusive tracks through the treacherous Himalayan terrain, encountering the testimonies of mountaineers and local folklore that kept the spirit of this snow-covered cryptid alive.

Venturing further south, we unravelled the enigmatic presence of the Orang Pendek, a mysterious creature that roams the dense rainforests of Sumatra. Eyewitness accounts and the tales of local villagers provided glimpses into the hidden world of this elusive ape-like being, challenging us to reconsider our assumptions about what lies hidden in the depths of the wilderness.

From there, we embarked on a thrilling adventure into the remote regions of Mongolia, where the awe-inspiring Death

Worm resides beneath the vast expanses of the Gobi Desert. Uncovering ancient accounts and modern expeditions, we delved into the mysterious folklore surrounding this cryptid and pondered the origins of its terrifying powers.

The monstrous, serpentine creature known as the Naga drew us deeper into the rich mythology of Southeast Asia. From the shimmering waters of the Mekong River to the dense jungles of Laos, we explored the ancient temples and sacred sites associated with this divine creature, provoking wonder and curiosity about its existence.

Our journey through Asia's cryptid tapestry also brought us face to face with the Baku, a fantastical creature believed to devour nightmares in Japanese folklore. We encountered its enigmatic presence in the shadowy realm of dreams, delving into the depths of the human subconscious and pondering the possibilities of such an extraordinary being.

From the enigmatic depths of the sea, the sea serpents known as the Umibōzu lured us into the tumultuous waters of the Pacific Ocean. Sailors' tales and folklore guided our quest to unravel the secrets of these colossal creatures, inspiring both awe and caution as we contemplated their vast and mysterious existence beneath the waves.

Our exploration continued into the verdant landscapes of Vietnam, where the elusive Rock Apes dwell in the towering limestone karsts. Engaging with local accounts and venturing into the heart of these majestic landscapes, we marvelled at the possibility of undiscovered primate species inhabiting these untouched realms.

From the dense forests of Malaysia, we were drawn into the captivating world of the Penanggalan, a fearsome female vampire who detaches her head from her body in search of blood. With a shiver down our spines, we explored the dark depths of this folklore, contemplating the origins and symbolism of this terrifying legend.

The majestic Qilin led us further into the realm of mythical creatures, captivating us with its grace and wisdom. We traversed ancient scrolls and unearthed artwork depicting this mythical beast, tracing its footsteps through the rich cultural history of China and marvelling at the symbolism and significance it holds within.

Lastly, we delved into the depths of the legendary Hoan Kiem Turtle, residing within the serene waters of Hoan Kiem Lake in Vietnam. Immersed in the tales of its revered status and supernatural abilities, we contemplated the spiritual connection between humans and the natural world, allowing the allure of this mythical creature to envelop our senses.

And so, as our expedition comes to a close, we are left with a profound appreciation for the rich tapestry of Asia's cryptid lore. Each step we took, each tale we unravelled, brought us closer to understanding the intricate relationship between myth and reality, between the human imagination and the untamed wilderness.

Throughout this journey, we have witnessed the power of storytelling, the way it weaves together the threads of history, culture, and belief. These cryptids are not mere figments of imagination; they are a reflection of the human desire to explore the unknown, to seek answers to the mysteries that surround us.

In our quest to uncover the truth behind these cryptids, we have encountered scepticism and scepticism. Yet, it is this very scepticism that drives us to question, to investigate, and to push the boundaries of what we think we know. For within the realm of the unexplained lies the potential for discovery, for new understandings of the world we inhabit.

As we bid farewell to the top ten cryptids of Asia, we carry with us the memories of awe-inspiring landscapes, the whispers of ancient legends, and the stories shared by those who believe. Our journey has been one of exploration, not only of the physical world but also of the human imagination and its enduring connection to the natural world.

May these tales continue to captivate the hearts and minds of generations to come, inspiring future explorers and researchers to venture into the depths of the unknown. For in the pursuit of these cryptids, we are reminded of the infinite wonders that await us, the mysteries that beckon us to seek answers, and the enduring power of the human spirit to embrace the enigmatic.

As we conclude this chapter, we invite you to carry the spirit of adventure and curiosity with you, to embark on your own quest, whether it be in the realms of myth and legend or in the unexplored corners of our own reality. For within the unknown lies the promise of discovery, and within discovery lies the opportunity to expand our understanding of the world and ourselves.

May the cryptids of Asia continue to ignite our imagination, reminding us that there is always more to explore, to learn, and to marvel at in this vast and wondrous world. Farewell, dear reader, until our paths cross again, in the pages of another extraordinary journey.

Cryptids, with their rich cultural, scientific, and ecological significance, play a fascinating role in the lives of local communities. Let us delve into each aspect and explore their impact.

Cultural Significance

CRYPTIDS ARE DEEPLY rooted in the cultural fabric of societies, often existing as legends, folklore, and mythical creatures passed down through generations. They embody the collective imagination and belief systems of communities, offering a connection to ancestral heritage and a sense of identity. Cryptids become part of the cultural narrative, shaping rituals, art, literature, and celebrations. They can symbolise various aspects of local traditions, values, and fears, carrying a profound meaning that transcends time.

These creatures inspire storytellers, artists, and musicians, who weave their tales into the cultural tapestry. They become characters in epic sagas, cautionary tales, and moral fables, imparting wisdom and reflecting societal beliefs. By preserving the legends of cryptids, communities ensure the preservation of their cultural heritage, passing down these stories as a legacy to future generations.

Scientific Significance

CRYPTIDS SPARK SCIENTIFIC curiosity and provide avenues for exploration and discovery. They challenge our understanding of the natural world and push the boundaries of scientific inquiry. The quest to uncover evidence of cryptids prompts researchers, cryptozoologists, and explorers to venture into remote and unexplored regions, often leading to the discovery of new species and ecological knowledge.

Even in cases where cryptids are eventually debunked, the process of investigation contributes to scientific learning. It encourages critical thinking, the gathering of empirical data, and the development of hypotheses. The study of cryptids fosters interdisciplinary collaboration, bringing together fields such as biology, zoology, anthropology, and environmental science. It encourages researchers to examine the unknown, leading to advancements in our understanding of the diversity of life on Earth.

Ecological Significance

CRYPTIDS CAN ALSO HAVE significant ecological implications. Local communities living in areas inhabited by cryptids often develop a unique relationship with their natural surroundings. These creatures become symbols of the biodiversity and fragile ecosystems they are believed to inhabit. Cryptids can inspire conservation efforts as communities recognize the importance of preserving their habitats and the delicate balance of nature.

The pursuit of cryptids can shed light on previously unknown or endangered species. Expeditions and investigations focused on cryptids often involve extensive exploration of remote regions, resulting in the documentation of rare flora and fauna. By promoting the conservation of habitats that support cryptids, we indirectly protect the broader ecosystems they are a part of, safeguarding biodiversity and preserving ecological balance.

Additionally, cryptids can also serve as flagship species, attracting attention and resources for conservation initiatives. They raise public awareness about the importance of protecting natural habitats, fostering environmental stewardship, and encouraging sustainable practices.

Cryptids have a multifaceted impact on local communities. They contribute to cultural heritage, ignite scientific curiosity, and promote ecological conservation. As we navigate the intersection of folklore, science, and environmental consciousness, the significance of these enigmatic beings continues to captivate our imagination, reminding us of the intricate connections between humanity, nature, and the wonders that lie hidden within our world.

Despite the extensive exploration and research conducted on cryptids, many mysteries and unanswered questions persist, shrouding these enigmatic creatures in an air of intrigue and fascination. Let us delve into some of these ongoing mysteries that continue to captivate the minds of researchers and enthusiasts alike.

Existence and Elusiveness

THE PRIMARY QUESTION surrounding cryptids is their existence. While eyewitness testimonies, cultural beliefs, and alleged sightings provide compelling anecdotes, concrete scientific evidence remains elusive. Cryptids often inhabit remote and inaccessible regions, making it challenging to obtain verifiable evidence such as clear photographs, DNA samples, or physical remains. The elusive nature of these creatures raises questions about their true existence and the possibility of their continued survival in the face of human encroachment.

Taxonomic Classification

IF A CRYPTID IS PROVEN to exist, its taxonomic classification becomes an intriguing puzzle. Determining the evolutionary origins, genetic makeup, and ecological role of these creatures would contribute significantly to our understanding of biodiversity. However, the lack of tangible evidence makes it difficult to place cryptids within existing taxonomic frameworks. Discovering new species or uncovering the existence of evolutionary outliers could challenge established scientific knowledge and redefine our understanding of the natural world.

Cultural and Psychological Significance

CRYPTIDS HOLD IMMENSE cultural and psychological significance, but the underlying reasons for their enduring presence in human folklore and belief systems remain enigmatic. Why do these particular creatures capture our imagination? What psychological or societal factors contribute to their creation and perpetuation? Exploring the cultural and psychological dimensions of cryptids could shed light on the human propensity for myth-making, the power of storytelling, and the ways in which beliefs shape our perception of the world.

Ecological Interactions

CRYPTIDS OFTEN OCCUPY specific ecological niches within their respective habitats, and understanding their ecological interactions is crucial for comprehending the delicate balance of ecosystems. Unanswered questions revolve around the potential ecological roles of cryptids, their impact on prey populations, and their interdependence with other species. Exploring these interactions could provide valuable insights into the functioning and resilience of ecosystems, as well as inform conservation efforts.

Cryptid Origins and Evolution

THE ORIGINS AND EVOLUTION of cryptids are subjects of intrigue and speculation. Are they relics of ancient lineages that have managed to survive against the odds? Could they be undiscovered species, representing unique branches on the tree of life? Exploring the evolutionary history of cryptids would unravel their place within the larger tapestry of life on Earth, offering insights into adaptive strategies, genetic diversity, and the mechanisms that drive speciation.

Cryptids as Guardians of the Unknown

CRYPTIDS EMBODY THE mysteries that continue to elude us, serving as guardians of the unknown. While scientific inquiry strives to unravel these mysteries, the existence of cryptids reminds us of the boundless wonders that remain hidden in the unexplored corners of our world. They beckon us to maintain a sense of wonder and curiosity, to push the boundaries of knowledge, and to embrace the enigmatic aspects of our existence.

As we navigate the realm of cryptids, these ongoing mysteries remind us that the pursuit of knowledge is a journey that often raises more questions than answers. The allure of these enigmatic creatures continues to inspire exploration, spark scientific inquiry, and capture the imagination of generations to come. The quest to uncover the truth behind cryptids represents a testament to our innate human curiosity and the ceaseless pursuit of understanding the mysteries that lie beyond our current knowledge.

In the face of the enduring mysteries and unanswered questions surrounding cryptids, there is a profound need for further research, exploration, and open-mindedness. The exploration of these enigmatic creatures offers a gateway to uncharted territories, both in the physical world and within our collective understanding.

To unravel the secrets hidden within the realms of cryptids, we must continue to encourage scientific inquiry and interdisciplinary collaboration. Researchers, cryptozoologists, and explorers should be supported in their endeavours to venture into remote and unexplored regions, armed with the latest technologies and methodologies. Expeditions should be organised with meticulous planning, combining traditional fieldwork with cutting-edge scientific techniques, ensuring the collection of reliable data and evidence.

An open-minded approach is essential when examining the possibilities surrounding cryptids. We must be willing to challenge preconceived notions and biases, embracing the potential for new discoveries and paradigm shifts in our understanding of the natural world. This requires the inclusion of diverse perspectives, knowledge systems, and cultural beliefs, recognizing that the exploration of cryptids transcends individual disciplines and encompasses a broader tapestry of human experience.

Furthermore, technological advancements offer unprecedented opportunities for research and investigation. High-resolution cameras, DNA analysis, remote sensing techniques, and advanced data collection methods can provide valuable insights into the existence and characteristics of cryptids. Leveraging these tools in a systematic and rigorous manner can contribute to the accumulation of concrete evidence and further our understanding of these enigmatic beings.

It is crucial to maintain a sense of wonder, curiosity, and humility. Cryptids remind us that the world is vast and filled with wonders yet to be discovered. They invite us to embrace the unknown, to appreciate the complexity of our natural surroundings, and to recognize our place within a grander ecosystem.

Let us encourage and support further research into cryptids, fostering an environment that nurtures scientific exploration, cultural understanding, and ecological conservation. By doing so, we can unravel the secrets hidden within the realms of cryptids, unravelling the enigmatic stories that have captivated our imaginations for generations and expanding our understanding of the intricate web of life on our remarkable planet.

The enduring allure of cryptids lies in their ability to capture the human imagination and evoke a sense of wonder, mystery, and curiosity. From generation to generation, across cultures and continents, the fascination with the unknown has persisted, and cryptids embody that timeless fascination in a profound way.

At the heart of our collective fascination with cryptids is the innate human desire to explore and understand the world around us. The allure of the unknown beckons us to venture into uncharted territories, both physically and intellectually. Cryptids represent a gateway to the enigmatic, to realms where science and myth intertwine, challenging our preconceptions and expanding the boundaries of our knowledge.

Cryptids tap into the deep recesses of our imagination, awakening our sense of awe and igniting our thirst for discovery. They embody the untamed wilderness and the mysteries that lie within it. These elusive creatures tantalise us with the possibility of hidden wonders, unexplained phenomena, and uncharted realms waiting to be explored.

Additionally, cryptids embody the triumph of curiosity and the human spirit of adventure. They inspire us to question, to search for answers, and to challenge conventional wisdom. The pursuit of cryptids is not just a quest for physical evidence; it represents a profound intellectual and emotional journey, urging us to explore the boundaries of what we know and to embrace the tantalising possibilities of what we don't.

Moreover, cryptids resonate with our cultural narratives and belief systems. They become part of our collective folklore, passed down through generations, and intertwined with our identity and heritage. These creatures embody the wisdom of our ancestors, the traditions that have shaped our communities, and the enduring power of storytelling. They serve as a bridge between the tangible and the intangible, the known and the unknown, connecting us to a deeper understanding of our place in the world.

The enduring allure of cryptids also lies in their capacity to spark our sense of awe and reverence for the natural world. In an era where technological advancements have made the world seem smaller and more comprehensible, cryptids remind us that there are still mysteries waiting to be unravelled. They remind us that the vastness of our planet is still filled with hidden corners, unexplored habitats, and species yet to be discovered. Cryptids represent the embodiment of the wild, the untamed, and the unpredictable aspects of nature, challenging our assumptions and inviting us to embrace the diversity and complexity of the living world.

The enduring allure of cryptids stems from the deep-seated human fascination with the unknown. They captivate our imagination, inspire our sense of adventure, and spark our intellectual curiosity. Cryptids remind us of the mysteries that lie beyond our current understanding, inviting us to embrace the enigmatic and to continue our unending quest to explore, discover, and comprehend the wonders of our world.

In the captivating realm of Asia's cryptid legends, a treasure trove of cultural richness and diversity awaits those who seek to delve into the mysteries of the natural world. These ancient tales, steeped in the traditions of diverse communities, offer a profound glimpse into the intricacies of human imagination and the enduring connection between culture and nature.

Let these cryptid legends serve as a gateway to the vibrant tapestry of Asia's cultural heritage. Embrace the enchanting stories passed down through generations, the legends whispered in hushed tones, and the awe-inspiring creatures that inhabit the collective consciousness of communities across the continent. Each cryptid embodies a unique aspect of cultural identity, reflecting the values, fears, and aspirations of those who have woven them into the fabric of their traditions.

In exploring the hidden wonders within Asia's cryptid lore, we embark on a journey that extends beyond the realms of myth and legend. We are invited to appreciate the diversity of beliefs, the richness of storytelling, and the interconnectedness of humanity with the natural world. It is a call to honour the wisdom of our ancestors and the ways in which they found solace, wonder, and guidance in the mysteries that surround us.

Beyond the captivating narratives lies a deeper connection to the natural world. Asia's cryptids are intertwined with the region's awe-inspiring landscapes, from lush rainforests to snow-capped mountains and from pristine lakes to remote islands. These creatures are a testament to the ecological richness and diversity that make Asia a cradle of life. They invite us to appreciate the fragile balance of ecosystems and to become stewards of the environments that support both the known and the unknown.

As we immerse ourselves in the cultural tapestry of Asia's cryptid legends, let us embrace a spirit of open-mindedness, curiosity, and respect. Let us celebrate the diversity of beliefs and interpretations, recognizing that each community brings a unique perspective and understanding to these tales. By engaging with these legends, we foster a deeper appreciation for cultural heritage, cultivating empathy, and fostering cross-cultural connections.

Furthermore, the exploration of cryptids invites us to continue our quest for hidden wonders in the natural world. Let us embark on expeditions, both literal and metaphorical, to the remote and unexplored corners of our planet. As we navigate the uncharted territories, we forge new paths of discovery, unravelling the enigmas that lie hidden in the depths of forests, mountains, and oceans.

In our pursuit of hidden wonders, we are reminded of the vastness of our world and the interconnectedness of all life. We are inspired to preserve the habitats that harbour these mysteries, advocating for the conservation of ecosystems and the protection of biodiversity. By embracing the exploration of hidden wonders, we become advocates for the natural world, nurturing a sense of awe, respect, and responsibility for the environments we inhabit.

So let us embark on this journey of exploration, celebration, and conservation. Let us appreciate the cultural richness and diversity of Asia's cryptid legends, honouring the stories that have shaped communities for generations. And let us continue to discover the hidden wonders that await us in the natural world, for in doing so, we deepen our connection to the Earth and nurture our own sense of wonder, humility, and appreciation for the extraordinary world in which we live.

Don't miss out!

Visit the website below and you can sign up to receive emails whenever Edward Turner publishes a new book. There's no charge and no obligation.

https://books2read.com/r/B-A-SYIZ-OSKLC

BOOKS2READ

Connecting independent readers to independent writers.

Also by Edward Turner

Ghosts of Paris: Ten Haunted Places in the City of Love
Asia's Top Ten Cryptids: Legends, Sightings, and Theories
Evil Women in History: Uncovering the Gruesome Crimes of
Ten Notorious Female Killers
Ghosts of London: Ten Haunted Places in The City
Ghosts of New York: Ten Haunted Places in The Big Apple
North America's Top Ten Cryptids: Legends, Sightings, and
Theories

About the Author

Edward Turner is a renowned author who specializes in exploring the realms of ghosts, the paranormal, and cryptids. With a captivating writing style and an insatiable curiosity for the unknown, Turner has garnered a dedicated following of readers who are captivated by his thrilling and eerie tales.

Born with an innate fascination for the supernatural, Turner has spent decades delving into the depths of paranormal phenomena, unearthing captivating stories and untangling mysteries that lie beyond the veil of the ordinary. His extensive research and meticulous attention to detail have earned him a reputation as a leading authority in the field.

Through his books, Turner expertly weaves together chilling accounts of encounters with ghosts, offering readers a glimpse into the ethereal world that coexists alongside our own. His ability to paint vivid portraits of spectral apparitions and convey the haunting atmosphere of haunted locations has made his works both spine-tingling and thought-provoking.

Turner's exploration of the paranormal doesn't stop at ghosts. He also dives into the fascinating world of cryptids—creatures that defy conventional explanation. His in-depth investigations into legendary creatures such as Bigfoot, the Loch Ness Monster, and the Chupacabra showcase his commitment to shedding light on these enigmatic beings.

With each page, Edward Turner's readers are drawn deeper into the enigmatic and unknown. His unique storytelling ability combined with his meticulous research has made him a sought-after author for those with an insatiable thirst for the supernatural. Whether delving into ghostly encounters or unraveling the mysteries of elusive cryptids, Turner's books offer a spine-chilling and immersive reading experience that leaves readers questioning the boundaries of our reality.

Edward Turner's works have earned critical acclaim and numerous accolades within the paranormal genre. He continues to explore the unexplained, captivating readers with his distinctive narrative style and unwavering dedication to unveiling the mysteries that lie hidden in the shadows.